THE FREE PRESS

New York   London   Toronto   Sydney   Singapore

Executive Summary

An increasing number of big companies in Western countries—especially the US—are breaking themselves up. Some are "demerging" or "spinning off" divisions and subsidiaries. Others are breaking themselves up into three or four separate pieces, and simultaneously eliminating the corporate center.

The scale of this movement is staggering. In the US, the market value of spin-offs is now at an annual level of $100 billion, i.e., more than the leveraged buyout (LBO) boom at its height in 1989. The pace has been increasing since the early 1980s. It now seems like an irreversible tide.

Many explanations have been offered: management focus, the desirability of getting a "fair share price," the necessity to reduce debt, the prospect of eliminating competitive conflict within the corporation, and even that this is all just another management fad.

There is little question that all of these factors contribute to the trend. But none of them explains why there is money to be made from breaking companies up, or why, when a breakup is rumored or announced, the share price shoots up. To understand the real reason for breakups, we need to explain why there is money on the table.

Companies are worth more dead than alive because of value destruction. Value destruction is a pervasive, often irresistible, force in Multibusiness Companies (MBCs). Because of the existence of a corporate center, and because of friction between business units, the overall performance of a multibusiness portfolio is often less than the performance would be if the business units were independent. The difference is not small. We estimate that between 10 percent and 50 percent of value is destroyed by the formation of a multibusiness organization.

Does this mean that all MBCs should break up? No. Some create enough value to offset the value destruction. Some are net value creators. These Focused Business Companies (FBCs) have two common features.

First, they have corporate-center skills, resources, and knowledge that are valuable to the businesses. These skills help the businesses improve performance by a substantial amount (20 percent or more).

Second, FBCs keep value destruction to a minimum by limiting their portfolios to "similar" businesses: businesses that have similar critical success factors. There are many ways that large corporations can add value to the businesses in their portfolios. Unfortunately there are just as many ways for them to destroy value. Despite the best efforts of well-intentioned executives at the center, value destruction is very hard to avoid. We explain why. Unless the center can add more value than it destroys, the businesses suffer from being a part of the larger whole. In our experience, this net value destruction happens more often than not.

Companies can decide whether breakup should be on their own agenda by asking four questions: What are the natural clusters or groupings of businesses in the current portfolio? Which of these clusters fit best with the corporate center's skills and resources? Is there a value creating reason for keeping the clusters together in one multicluster company? Does the value creating reason stand up to challenge?

In our experience all MBCs will benefit from asking these questions and, having answered them, more than half will benefit from breaking up or, at a minimum, spinning off part of their portfolios. Currently, too many companies view breakup as a last resort: an admission of failure. For many it would be a positive step to create two or more companies from the original one. They would generate more valuable, more focused jobs for their senior managers; and they would release more energy and commitment from their organizations. Breakup, where it is needed, should be viewed as one of the more attractive corporate strategy options.

Yet breaking up is hard to do. Companies wanting to break up need to take care. Expect emotional resistance. Focus on the positives, particularly the performance improvement, that can be expected after breakup. Create a "credo" to help manage the process. Appoint a project manager. Execute the process quickly. Communicate throughout. Recognize that it is a big job. These are all lessons learned from experience.

The breakup epidemic heralds a new era of capitalism. The future will bring a new industrial landscape. Gone will be all but a few of today's sprawling MBCs. Gone will be management's attachment to size. Gone will be the ambition of the generalist manager seeking to apply his or her skills like a professional. Gone will be objectives such as risk-spreading, balance, a third leg to the stool, and other management fallacies.

In the new landscape there will be more single businesses, more FBCs, and more value creation. At least a trillion dollars more—$1,000,000,000,000—by our estimates.

We expect the new landscape to change some bulwarks of capitalism. There will be fewer mergers and acquisitions as the seemingly endless game of pass-the-parcel between diversified companies comes to an end. Institutions will increasingly invest for the long term, choosing the management teams they want to back, and sticking with their decisions. Even management career paths will change. Ambitious individuals will aim to be specialists, not generalists, and will mainly focus on one industry or functional area, proud of honing their skills, rather than wistfully seeking an invitation into the club of so-called general managers.

Big changes are under way in our commercial landscape. The breakup epidemic is a signal of how big the changes will be.

Authors' Note

T his book is deliberately opportunist. We have been watching with excitement the growing number of breakups—companies choosing to spin off or demerge substantial parts of their portfolios. We could see the link between breakup and its forerunners—management buyouts (MBOs), leveraged buyouts (LBOs), hostile takeovers, and deconglomeration. We could sense that breakup is part of a positive move by managers to be in charge of their company's destiny. We therefore wanted to be the first to explain breakup and to celebrate the impact it will have on management thinking.

We also wanted to write about breakup as a vehicle for promoting our views on corporate-level strategy, diversified companies, and the role of corporate centers. Breakups—decisions to make companies smaller in order to make them more effective—need an explanation, particularly at a time when we still admire bigness. Most managers grow up wanting to make their companies larger. There must be, therefore, some unusual forces at work to persuade managers voluntarily to make their companies smaller. We believe we understand why this is happening and what it means for the future of big business and capitalism at large.

The phrase "our views on corporate-level strategy" needs to be expanded, because our thinking is greatly influenced by the research and writings of the Ashridge Strategic Management Centre in London. The Ashridge work has been widely published in books and articles. The term "parenting advantage" has been coined by Ashridge to describe the objective of good corporate-level strategy. The Ashridge work is even sometimes referred to as "parenting theory"—the theory that guides the behavior of the corporate parent. This research, led by Michael Goold, Andrew Campbell, and Marcus

Alexander, provided the basic insights into why multibusiness companies (MBCs) can destroy value, and the methodology for analyzing whether a particular company should be broken up. The Ashridge research is most fully documented in *Corporate-Level Strategy: Creating Value in the Multibusiness Company* by Michael Goold, Andrew Campbell, and Marcus Alexander. (John Wiley & Son, 1994)

Breakup! draws deeply on the Ashridge research, but there are differences.

First, we use different terminology. We have avoided the parenting theory language, partly because we have made some minor modifications to the Ashridge concepts and partly to avoid the parenting jargon.

Second, we present both a more provocative and a looser message than that contained in the Ashridge work. This is not primarily a research-based book. It is a collection of observations, ideas, and beliefs. We are not seeking precision and proof. We are seeking insight and implication. This is a popular rather than a theoretical book.

Our message is more provocative because the breakup trend exposes the value destruction that lurks in many diversified companies; and we believe the trend will accelerate, exposing more value destruction than any previous research has identified. This has major implications for large companies, for management in general, and for capitalism. We speculate about these implications. Our views about the pervasiveness of value destruction and the implications this has for the future are our own, not those of Ashridge.

Our text is looser in its terminology and definition because we are seeking to communicate broad messages, not build a theory. We are writing a polemic, not a treatise. We are selling a point of view, not providing proof for our propositions.

Breakup, we believe, is a bold herald of a new way of thinking about MBCs. Not everyone agrees. Read on and make up your own mind.

David Sadtler
Andrew Campbell
Richard Koch
January 1997

Acknowledgments

W e wish to acknowledge three main debts: to the senior executives of corporations experiencing breakup; to our professional collaborators; and to our professional noncollaborators.

We have been fortunate in the generosity of our corporate interviewees. These busy people gave us their time and their unvarnished insights. We thank all those who have resisted, acquiesced in, and finally embraced, breakup for their corporations, and who relived for our benefit their expectations and emotions before, during, and after the breakup. We are, of course, particularly grateful to those who were open and who allowed us to quote them; but we are also deeply indebted to the others who faced a choice, and preferred being honest to being quoted.

And now our professional collaborators. We owe a significant debt to JP Morgan, the global bank, who was extremely helpful in our research and who allowed us to use its comprehensive data on US breakups. We owe even greater thanks to OC&C Strategy Consultants, who did such a sterling job on the Breakup 100 and who also provided a number of other insights into the breakup phenomenon. In particular, we salute Alex Fortescue and Chris Outram, who directed the OC&C work. We are also grateful to Simon Caulkin, for help in editing; and to Mark Allin, our publisher, who has helped to shape the book. To all other collaborators, please forgive our omission, and thank you too.

Third, thanks are due to Marcus Alexander and Michael Goold, Directors of the Ashridge Strategic Management Centre in London. They did not collaborate in the writing of the book, but they, together with Andrew Campbell, were the originators of the research, methodology, and insights about corporate strategy on which this book is largely based. Their critiques of the manuscript have taken off some of its raw edges and made it much better.

We acknowledge that the book could not have reached its current form without help from many intelligent and experienced people, but we take full responsibility for it.

Introduction

The Breakup Epidemic:
The Dismemberment of Big Business

The breakup epidemic will create enormous improvements in
company performance and, along with it, vastly increased
shareholder wealth.

In the breakup tidal wave, many managers will be swept
away; those who remain will have their work lives transformed, mainly
for the better. For shrewd investors, breakup offers the biggest
opportunity to get rich with low risk since the bull market of the 1980s.

C orporate America and corporate Britain are in the midst of an epidemic that will change the face of capitalism. In an unprecedented whirl-wind of self-dismemberment, companies, which used to believe that big is beautiful, are splitting into two, three, or more separate smaller companies. The Americans call it spin-off, and the British, demerger: we call it breakup.

The epidemic is good news. It will be the greatest wealth-producing change in management attitudes in our lifetimes. It will create enormous im-provements in company performance and, along with it, vastly increased shareholder wealth. Companies will produce better products, will serve their markets more responsively, and will be better places to work. Breakup is

1

bringing about a sea change in the way in which businesses are managed. In the long run, everyone will be the winner.

The movement began in the early 1990s but has already reached the "tipping point." It has rapidly accelerated to a point where its importance cannot be in doubt, and from where it will grow relentlessly until it has changed forever the theory and practice of big business. Although the facts are already evident, nobody has yet realized the significance of the breakup epidemic or even why it is taking place. Yet it will have a far bigger effect on society and on managers' lives than the delayering and downsizing of the early 1990s.

In the tidal wave, many managers will be swept away: those who remain will have their work lives transformed, mainly for the better. For shrewd investors, breakup offers the biggest opportunity to get rich with low risk since the bull market of the 1980s. It is good news for consumers: breakups enhance competitiveness, which ultimately creates customer value. For society, it could herald major social dislocation, although if the transition can be managed sensibly—by no means a safe conclusion—we should all benefit.

The scale of the phenomenon is shown in Figure 1. There has been a sudden and startling explosion of breakups. In 1993 the total value of companies spun off in the US and the UK ("breakoffs") was $17.5 billion; in 1994 it rose to $30 billion; and in 1995 shot up to a staggering $80 billion. In 1996 it advanced even further—to $91 billion. This contrasts with an average during the 1980s of less than $5 billion per year (see Figure 3 in Chapter 1 for a fifteen-year history).

In the space of less than a year, the most famous conglomerate in the United States, the largest American industrial corporation, the largest conglomerate and the largest public utility in Britain have all chosen to immolate themselves. The Continental Europeans, long averse to Anglo-Saxon corporate and financial engineering trends, are joining in. Lufthansa has spun off its air freight operations. Sandoz in Switzerland is spinning off its chemicals business. Sonae, the largest Portuguese retailer, is splitting up. Chargeurs, the French film and textile concern, is breaking itself into two pieces. All these large, respected, and long-successful companies have publicly admitted that they no longer have a right to exist in their previous form. Are Amer-

FIGURE 1

Breakoffs in the US and UK: Dollar Value of Transactions, 1992–95

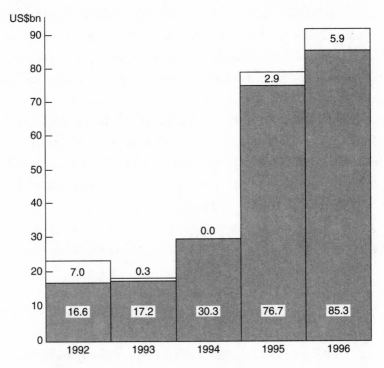

Source: IFR Securities Data

ican and European business empires in 1996–98 becoming the corporate equivalent of the Soviet Union and Eastern Europe in 1989–91? What on earth is going on?

$1 TRILLION MAY BE ON THE TABLE

Huge sums of money are at stake. The potential increase in wealth from harnessing the breakup revolution is almost frightening. Industrialists and investors who place themselves in the vanguard of the movement will make fortunes. Finding out why there is money on the table and then acting on that information will represent the single greatest wealth-creation opportunity available in the run-up to the next millennium.

These are the calculations. The total market capitalization of public companies in the United States and Britain is about $10 trillion, that is, $10,000 billion, or $10,000,000 million. The vast majority of these companies are in more than one line of business: what we call Multibusiness Companies (MBCs). As we shall see, at least half of all MBCs are probably eligible for a breakup (see Figure 2, which describes the results of an analysis of the largest companies in the US and the UK, and assesses their breakup potential); the methodology is discussed in the Appendix, which describes our Breakup 100. Experience to date indicates that a share price uplift of 20 percent, over and above any market increase, is a reasonable expectation for a breakup, even over a short period like eighteen months. If this were to happen for the population we have defined here, the total uplift potential could be as much as $1 trillion! And this is just for two of the world's stock markets. Whatever the value that is realized now, the longer term impact on the companies affected will be much greater.

However large the numbers, the real significance of breakup is not quantitative. It is the qualitative change in the nature of big business that really matters. For, although nobody has yet realized it, the breakup epidemic is not a fad, not the new fat cats' charter, not the last in a long line of corporate strategy fashions pronounced by management gurus to catch each spring's publishing season, not the most recent *deus ex machina* come to save those who head our great corporations and have run out of ideas for what to do next, and not the plaything of American investment bankers for whom billion-dollar deals are routine. Breakup certainly can be seen as any or all of the above, but to focus on these transient aspects of breakup would be to miss its revolutionary significance.

Look at the following two vignettes.

THE END OF ITT

ITT was the archetypal American conglomerate. The corporation became a financial superstar under the chairmanship of Harold Geneen, the legendary accountant. He led the company until 1977, but intended to set its struc-

FIGURE 2
Breakup Index: Summarized Results Showing the Breakup Potential of the
Largest US and UK Companies

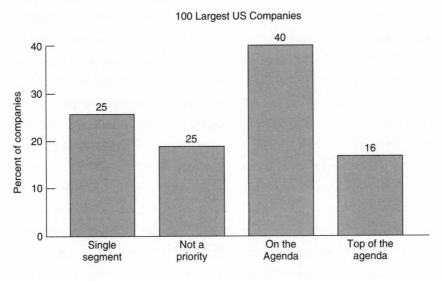

100 Largest US Companies

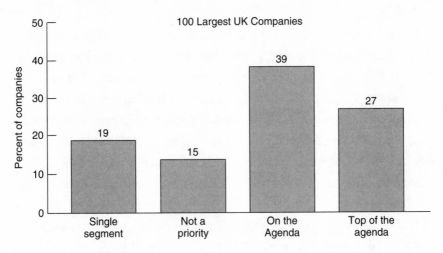

100 Largest UK Companies

Definitions

Top of the agenda: Breakup scores equal to or greater than the average of historic examples

On the agenda: Breakup scores equal to or greater than the lowest of historic examples

Not a priority: Breakup scores lower than the lowest of historic examples

Single segment: Subsidiary business units less than 10 percent of turnover

ture, shape, and culture in concrete. In the 1960s and 1970s, ITT represented the successful, financially driven, tightly controlled conglomerate. Geneen had two aims: safety through diversification, a lack of dependence on any one business; and the establishment of a numbers-led machine to wring higher margins and returns on capital out of all the businesses within the ITT empire. The formula worked on any business. Acquisitions were made in any industry. ITT could raise the profits of any business.

Geneen's formula worked. Relentlessly, quarter after quarter, the company raised earnings per share. Moreover, such was his faith in the machine he had built that Geneen believed the process could carry on forever. "After I leave," he boasted, "a monkey will be able to run this place."

After a brief stopgap, Geneen was succeeded, not by a monkey, but by Rand Araskog. During his tenure, Araskog responded to the ideology of the times that urged a focus on core businesses. He narrowed the scope of ITT, selling some 200 companies. Nonetheless, ITT remained a conglomerate of enormous range, and it continued to grow. By 1995, revenues had reached $24 billion.

But ITT had long since stopped being a stock-market darling. Earnings per share had stalled, conglomerates were out of fashion, and analysts distrusted ITT's complex financial maneuverings. In 1994, articles surfaced in the business press suggesting the desirability of a breakup. Investors were beginning to reap the benefits of demergers and spin-offs from corporations that, like ITT, seemed to be in too many businesses. ITT was a perfect subject for the new medicine. The rumors intensified when Araskog's pay package was redesigned to focus his attention on the ITT stock price.

In June 1995, the board of ITT announced its plans to break up the company. ITT was to be split into three successor companies: insurance (accounting for roughly one half of ITT's profits); leisure, incorporating hotels and casinos; and ITT Industries, the receptacle for its other, mainly manufacturing, businesses.

The market loved the plan. The shares raced ahead some 30 percent. Araskog's volte-face preserved his job, enabled him to escape mandatory retirement at age 65, and cast him in the light of a pragmatist, a statesman, and an exemplary steward of stockholder interests (not to mention his own). The biggest and most watched conglomerate, the *ne plus ultra* of the multibusiness company, the legacy of Harold Geneen, had finally succumbed. Others would follow.

SEARS ROEBUCK: A RETURN TO ITS ROOTS

By contrast to ITT, Sears built its size and reputation in one business: catalogue and in-store retailing. Its aggressive expansion into "related" businesses is what caused the trouble.

In the 1950s and 1960s, Sears had expanded its retail store network until there was a Sears outlet in every major community. In the 1960s and 1970s, Sears began to diversify its merchandise lines and started to enter new businesses. The chairman until 1993, Edward Brennan, championed diversification and in the 1980s led Sears into a major effort in financial services.

Brennan's idea was that of one stop shopping. He added a brokerage firm (Dean Witter) and a real estate concern (Coldwell Banker) to Allstate, Sears' insurance operation. He believed that Sears' loyal customers would buy houses, insurance, and stocks and bonds from a single financial services outlet. At about this time, a number of other large service organizations (American Express, Prudential, Merrill Lynch, etc.) were trying to create similar one stop shops. It just didn't work. Buying everything under one roof sounded like a fantastic synergy idea, but it proved less attractive to the public.

Sears made three big mistakes: (1) one stop financial shopping was a bad idea; (2) the debt incurred, largely to buy these businesses ($52 billion), sapped strategic flexibility; and (3) perhaps most importantly, it diverted the attention of Sears management from the mainstream retailing business. Throughout the 1980s, Sears had lost market share to more aggressive full-line merchandise retailers like Wal-Mart and K-Mart and to specialized retailers like Toys-'R'-Us.

The breakup that followed was one of the most successful in American history. Allstate's spin-off valued the business at a colossal $8.7 billion. During this same year, Sears sold Dean Witter and Coldwell Banker, reducing debt by $20 billion. Sears' real estate development subsidiary, Homart Development, followed in 1995 and its share of Prodigy, the on-line computer service joint venture with IBM, was sold in 1996.

The solution for the retail side was to bring in new blood. Arthur Martinez was hired from up-market Saks Fifth Avenue to turn the ailing retail operations around. Martinez was a whirlwind of activity. He shut down the catalogue business, an emotionally wrenching decision for old Sears hands. He closed stores. He eliminated 50,000 jobs.

Sears retail operations are now improving. After years of deteriorating performance and a $2.9 billion loss in 1992, profits rebounded to $0.7 billion in 1993, $0.9 billion in 1994, and $1.3 billion in 1995. Sales, both in total and per store, are up, as are margins and customer traffic. The turnaround has been little short of remarkable.

Returning to its roots has been the right decision for Sears. The total market capitalization of the company had sunk to $8 billion in 1990. By the end of 1995, after the disposals and spin-offs and after new management had turned around the retail business, total capitalization of Sears and all the pieces had risen to $42 billion.

THE REASONS STATED OR SOMETHING MORE?

We know the reasons for these gigantic transactions. Rand Araskog had his eye on the ITT share price and on his cost of capital. Sears needed to get its debts under control and fund a revitalization of the heritage retailing business. But what was really going on at ITT and Sears? Why did it make financial sense to break them up? Why was there a large amount of value waiting to be released—30 percent at ITT and a five-times increase in shareholder wealth from 1990 to 1995?

While the breakup phenomenon has captured the attention of many, few have stopped to ask why it is happening. Even fewer have supplied satisfactory answers.

Conventional explanations of breakup are inadequate or misleading.

Some argue that breakups happen because managers need to focus limited resources. Others assert that it's all about hyping the share price, or (if they are managers or investors) "getting a fair market valuation." Lawyers and accountants talk about the tax efficiency of breakup as an alternative to major sales of assets or subsidiaries. The cynics tell you that it's a device to avoid takeover, or that it's just another financial reengineering fad. Each of these explanations captures a sliver of the truth, but they all miss the main point.

THE FUTURE IS FOCUS

The future is clear. The traditional MBC is a dinosaur. It will be replaced by two types of organizations. The single business is a familiar animal. Most MBCs started life as single businesses and need to break up in order to recreate the focus of a single business. McDonald's is a single business. Intel is a single business.

The Focused Business Company (FBC) is less familiar. The FBC is a multibusiness organization, but it is focused on one set of corporate center skills. In an FBC, the corporate center has a set of skills or resources that add value to each of its businesses. Procter & Gamble is an FBC. Disney is an FBC. 3M, since its breakup, is an FBC. Each has earned its FBC credentials; each has built a company around a set of central skills and capabilities that can create value across the portfolio of businesses.

Good breakups create single businesses and FBCs. Bad breakups create more MBCs or leave behind a rump that is still an MBC. 3M is a good breakup; ITT's breakup is good in parts but some MBCs still remain.

VALUE DESTRUCTION IS THE REASON FOR BREAKUP

Every MBC is a mixture of value creation and value destruction. Value creation comes in the form of innovations in technology, products, and services; more satisfied customers, and hence market share gains; international expansion; and investment in management development. Value creation comes from the vitality and skills of the managers running the businesses;

from their know-how, market presence, customer base, and commitment to improvements in quality and value for money. It can also come from the skill of the center in orchestrating this performance. In FBCs, the value thus created can be enormous. The efforts of business unit managers are multiplied by the skills of the center, and success abounds.

But in most MBCs value creation is accompanied by value destruction. Value destruction derives from the existence of a corporate center and from the friction between unnatural bedfellows within the corporation. Value destruction eats away at value creation. Rather than 2 plus 2 being more than 4, it becomes less than 4 (or less than 3!). Value destruction is the reason for breakup. Only by understanding its root causes can a new breed of FBCs rise from the growing pile of MBC husks.

Ten years of research conducted by the Ashridge Strategic Management Centre has shown that many MBCs systematically destroy value. The Ashridge research—published in *Strategies and Styles* (Michael Goold and Andrew Campbell, Blackwell, 1987) and *Corporate-Level Strategy* (Michael Goold, Andrew Campbell, and Marcus Alexander, Wiley, 1994)—was aimed at finding successful models that could be used to help today's MBCs. And the researchers found such models: the FBCs (companies like Emerson, 3M, Canon, ABB, and RTZ).

But the overwhelming conclusion, one applauded by every middle-management audience it is presented to, and reinforced by the few model companies, is that most MBCs destroy value. One of the purposes of this book is to explain why value destruction is a pervasive force in large companies and why breakup is the ideal solution.

VALUE DESTRUCTION BY THE CENTER

The first cause of value destruction is the corporate center: the head office and/or other intermediaries between the providers of funds (banks and investors) and the operating companies.

This intermediary structure, the foundation of modern big business, was created to allow managers to diversify and still "manage." As recorded lovingly by the American business historian Alfred Chandler, the MBC was created by managers at General Motors and DuPont to cope with a problem. They were becoming overloaded. They couldn't handle all the decisions that were rising to the top. The answer: decentralize. Create business divisions: *invent the multibusiness company.*

With the invention, performance improved. The MBC proved to be a better way to organize. But what had really happened? The problem that managers at General Motors and DuPont faced was a value destruction problem. The people at the top were becoming a bottleneck. They were slowing things down, making poor decisions, not coping. By decentralizing, these companies reduced value destruction and the world proclaimed a victory for American management techniques.

This was no victory. This was a step back from disaster. Value destruction was reduced, but not by enough. And this new invention, the MBC, appeared to give a blessing to diversification. The center did not have to understand all its businesses well enough to make the decisions. It could divisionalize. It may be a coincidence but America started losing international competitiveness almost from the moment when the modern MBC concept was born.

In discovering the performance improvements that come from decentralization, managers never stopped to ask whether the performance improvements would be even greater if decentralization were to be taken to its obvious conclusion: breakup.

The corporate raiders of the 1980s—T. Boone Pickens, Hanson, and KKR, the leveraged buyout specialist—began exposing the MBC problem. The success of management buyouts and leveraged buyouts drove home the message. Many large corporations were destroying value. Their businesses were being held back, stifled, buried in red tape, smothered in management and led by administrators. Henry Kravis, a founder of KKR, explained his company's extraordinary success in these terms:

During the 1980s, buyouts became a powerful tool for badly needed corporate change—improving companies that had become bloated, unfocused and noncompetitive. Management buyouts addressed many of the problems created by the "professional manager." The boards appointed by these managers often let inefficiencies go unchallenged and allowed companies to lose focus, wasting corporate assets and eroding shareholder value.

The 1980s demonstrated that a corporate center is often not necessary. In fact the corporate center is often the problem.

Out of this realization has come new thinking; healthy thinking. Corporate centers don't have to exist. They should only exist if they bring some value to the businesses under their control. In an MBC, it is the center that must justify its existence, and it's a competitive world. Corporate centers are in competition with each other and with the marketplace. To survive in our economic jungle they have to be good. To justify their ownership of businesses, they have to be better at looking after their portfolio of businesses, and better at raising performance in their businesses, than any other corporate center could be.

Few pass this test by definition. Few corporate centers can be the best at what they do. But many centers don't even clear the first hurdle. They don't even beat the market. Their businesses would be better as independent companies. These are the true value destroyers. These are the companies that KKR and the other raiders have been stalking. These are today's breakup candidates.

VALUE DESTRUCTION FROM FRICTION

The second source of value destruction comes from friction. Like mismatched husbands and wives, businesses can hurt each other when brought together under a common roof.

Customers may refuse to buy from business A because it has a sister business that competes with those customers. This is what happened at AT&T. Suppliers are reluctant to work with business A because it has a sister business supplying similar products. This happened at Baxter International. Internal friction also cause problems. If you ask a roomful of managers how many prefer doing business with sister units rather than external businesses, they will vote one and all in favor of external relationships. Doing business within the family nearly always causes tensions.

Is this really a second source of value destruction, or is it the responsibility of the center to avoid destructive friction? Clearly it *is* a responsibility of the center: ultimately all fingers end up pointing at the managers in charge. But there are certain types of value destruction that stem from friction between businesses rather than from the antics of the center.

Traditionally, managers and academics alike have assumed that "synergy" between business units is the rationale for MBCs; that by coming together under common ownership businesses can more effectively work together, sharing knowledge and resources to the advantage of all. In the past this may have been true. Today it is generally not the case. An explosion of alliances, partnerships, joint ventures, and other special arrangements among independent businesses demonstrates that common ownership is not needed to secure synergy benefits. The costs of managing internal alliances and joint ventures are often greater than the costs of setting up familiar relationships between independent businesses. This fact of life led the recently retired head of planning at Shell International to coin the word "anergy" to describe synergy in reverse—value-destroying friction. As he says, "Anergy is more common than synergy in today's large companies."

BREAKUP: THE SOLUTION

Multibusiness companies suffer from the disease of value destruction. We are not talking here about the ability, dedication, or goodwill of managers within MBCs, either at the center or in the operating companies; we are not saying that managers are "failing" or "underperforming." We are saying that the multibusiness structure creates a situation where value destruction breeds. All other things being equal, businesses start to suffer and lose between 10 percent and 50 percent of their value if they are brought together under common ownership. This is a stark conclusion and one we will devote many pages to explaining.

The multibusiness organization can only make sense if there is sufficient value creation to offset the value destruction. In FBCs, this happens. In FBCs, the value destruction is low, closer to 10 percent than 50 percent, and the value creation is high. FBCs are the only form of multibusiness organizations that makes sense. The problem is that there are many old-style MBCs and few FBCs.

We estimate that more than half of today's large companies should have breakup on the agenda (see Figure 2 and the description of the Breakup 100 in the Appendix). In other words these companies own significant businesses that would perform better as independent companies.

The analysis of the Fortune 100 and the FTSE 100 has confirmed our research. The academic casework carried out at the Ashridge Strategic Management Centre and our personal consulting experience suggested that a large percentage of MBCs are overdiversified. The analysis by OC&C Strategy Consultants (presented in the Breakup 100) suggests that more than half of the large companies in the US and the UK are overdiversified. Fewer than a quarter are FBCs. The remainder are single businesses.

How do we change? How do we get from the current unhappy state to one where single businesses and FBCs dominate, and value destroying MBCs are a rarity? How do we grasp the trillion dollar opportunity?

Breakup (spinning off or demerging parts of the company) is not the only solution. Leveraged buyouts, management buyouts, or other ways of reducing stretch and creating focus can also address the problem. Corporate raiders and hostile takeovers can also mitigate value destruction, if the new owner can reduce or eliminate its worst aspects. Breakup is, however, often the fastest, easiest, most tax efficient, and, curiously, least revolutionary method. The shareholders and the managers (except those at the center) can remain the same after a breakup, yet enormous value is released simply by eliminating the source of value destruction. Hence the method's attraction.

We are excited about breakup. We believe it is not just *a* solution, but *the* solution. We believe breakup is going to transform our capitalist system.

Other solutions to value destruction are less attractive. The strategy pursued by many companies of exiting those parts of their portfolios they feel least comfortable with is a partial solution. Trade sales and management buyouts usually create value, but the original company remains intact. It has swapped some of its businesses for cash, with the intention of investing the cash in other businesses. The company's size ambitions have not changed, and its methods of operating have not been shaken up. The company has not really admitted to itself that value destruction is pervasive. It is trying to remake itself with evolution not revolution.

Raiders and hostile acquirers are more revolutionary, but they are fundamentally negative. Many companies have moved to protect themselves against raiders, backed sometimes by politicians at national or state level. The hostile acquisition is too blunt, too frightening, too negative a solution. Active shareholders, though often a great force for good, can also be counterproductive. They create boardroom dissonance, management resistance, and more negative undercurrents. They suck senior management into time-consuming governance processes and politics. They distract management from running the business. Active shareholders are trying to do the right thing, but often end up creating more heat than light.

BREAKUP FOR INSIDERS

Only breakup can be seen as positive by all parties. Only breakup results in revolution from the inside. Only breakup has few losers.

If you are the chairman of a breakup, it can be positive. You are likely to become chairman of two or more businesses instead of one. You can create two or more CEO jobs for your successors. You can create value for shareholders. You can create enthusiasm and motivation in the new businesses.

If you are a senior manager in the corporate center of a breakup, you may feel threatened. In most cases, however, the FBCs that are created by the breakup need your talents. Instead of a corporate center job where you have been trying to make sense of something that doesn't make sense, and justify your responsibilities when in your heart you have known they were not justifiable, you now have a real value-adding job, where you can use your skills to drive forward an FBC. You become appreciated, rather than avoided, by the businesses. You become fulfilled rather than frustrated.

If you are a division CEO or a business president, breakup is easily the most attractive solution. You have control. You are not sold to some unknown acquirer. Yet you are released from the burdensome center. You may become the head of an FBC or become one layer (or two layers) closer to the top of your company. You have more power and less pain.

Even if you are the corporate-level strategic planner, breakup can be seen as a positive influence on your life. The corporate planner could be the individual most threatened by breakup. Who needs a corporate planner when there is no corporate? Yet the corporate planner's job in an overstretched, overdiversified, value destroying MBC is the most soul-destroying job there is. We should know—we have been there and rubbed shoulders with those gallant individuals. In our experience, the corporate planner is usually pushing for a breakup. He or she knows better than most why the old-style MBC does not work.

GETTING IT RIGHT

Breakup is the only solution that can be positive for all. This is why it is spreading like wildfire. This is why breakup is the solution that will save us from sinking under the waves of value destruction. This is why breakup is the most important management invention since the multibusiness company.

Like all inventions, breakup can be mishandled. It is a management invention to deal with a problem: value destruction. Like the MBC solution before it, it can also fail to eliminate all the value destruction. A breakup into two or three pieces often results in two or three MBCs replacing the previous MBC. While the smaller MBCs normally perform better, they are still MBCs and should again be tested for value destruction. In many cases, managers of breakups find that the topic of breakup is back on the agenda within a few years. Why? Because the problem has not been fully grasped—old-fashioned thoughts about size, stability, or substance have crowded in on the purity of the breakup ideal. Successful breakups, ones that do not result in further breakups in ensuing years, root out all value destruction. Successful breakups acknowledge that value destruction is the enemy and they do not rest until all the value destruction has itself been destroyed.

Sumantra Ghoshal, the well-known Indian academic currently at the London Business School, likens the atmosphere of most MBCs to that of downtown Calcutta in summer. "It's oppressive. You feel drained of energy. New ideas all seem too difficult."

In contrast he describes the atmosphere of the woods outside Fontainebleau in France (the home of his previous business school—INSEAD): "You feel spring is permanently in the air. New ideas flow through you like electricity. Everything seems possible. You feel recharged."

While Sumantra's ideas of a good MBC differ from ours, the analogy still holds good. Breakup converts downtown Calcutta into the Fontainebleau woods. Most MBCs are downtown Calcutta. Well-run FBCs and single businesses are the woods of Fontainebleau.

THE FUTURE

The future we see has a radically changed landscape. Gone are all but a few of today's sprawling MBCs. Gone are mindsets wedded to size. Gone is the general management dream in which managers apply their skills like a profession. Gone is management's attachment to risk-spreading, balance, third legs to stools, and fourth legs to chairs.

In the new landscape, there will be many more single businesses. All major economies will have a thriving *Mittlestand,* the German name for the body of single businesses, mainly family owned, that have driven the German economy. The new landscape will still have multibusiness organizations, but in the form of FBCs rather than old-style MBCs.

The distinguishing mark of an FBC will be the quality of the rationale for its existence. Each FBC will have a powerful economic logic, rather than a cling-film description. Not all of this logic will be sound. Some will prove to be false. Some will be badly implemented. So there will still be breakups—breakups of failed FBCs. But in the new landscape, old-style MBCs, those with no value creating rationale, will be exposed by analysts, ridiculed by journalists, and hounded by shareholder activists.

The new landscape of focus does not necessarily mean industry focus. It means focus on value creation. Some FBCs will be highly diversified. Yet, like venture capitalists or leveraged buyout partnerships, they will make economic sense because of the skills of the corporate center. Each of their businesses will be benefiting from these skills and from the Fontainebleau atmosphere the center promotes.

Others will be focused on an industry or a piece of an industry, containing a cluster of businesses making similar products and selling to similar customers. Like single businesses, these companies will have special expertise in these products and markets, and they will have a culture that is uniquely suited to these businesses.

Both types of business have a focus; both are FBCs. The first has a focus around the special skills of the center. The second has a focus on core technical or market skills. Both will be creating value, and both will clearly understand, and avoid, the value destruction that lurks within the multibusiness organization structure.

BREAKUP, DIVERSIFICATION, AND ASIA

Breakup is an epidemic in the US, it has been important in the UK, and it is gathering momentum in Continental Europe, South Africa, and Australia. But, despite several newsworthy breakups, it has had little impact in Asia. In Asia, companies are still diversifying. In Korea, government efforts to break up the *chaebols,* large diverse groups that dominate 80 percent of the Korean economy, have failed. In Hong Kong, the conglomerates, with few exceptions, believe size counts. Size affords power; power they hope will provide security since the Chinese took back control in July 1997. In Southeast Asia, large family-controlled conglomerates continue to diversify, using their government relationships to enter new areas.

In an environment where "know-who" is more important than "know-how," where political influence is a source of advantage and where size breeds influence, diversification makes sense. Breakup is not the right medi-cine in all situations. Diversification can create and be driven by political in-fluence, preferential access to money, and a commanding share of the top talent. When it is, it creates value.

We could argue that Asian conglomerates are not really MBCs. They are FBCs. They are focused around some special skills of their centers—the cen-ter's know-who. But, however we put the argument, breakup is not yet re-quired in Asia.

As soon as Asian economies open their doors to pure market forces, as soon as their governments step back from their hands-on policies, as soon as the world's multinationals are allowed to compete on level terms, as soon as their capital markets become large enough to create a market in corporate control, then Asia will see the greatest breakup binge of all. The trends are moving in favor of breakup, but the binge won't happen until well into the next century.

But where government and industry deal with each other at arm's length and where capital markets and the market for corporate control hold man-agers to account, the breakup phenomenon will prosper and will create enor-mous value for owners, managers, and customers alike.

A GUIDE TO *BREAKUP!*

Chapter 1, The Epidemic Breaks Out, provides the hard facts about the growth of breakups. It shows where they have occurred, how they have grown, and the value of breakup in stock-market terms.

Chapter 2, What Drives Breakup?, deals more thoroughly with the causes of breakup. We analyze thirty landmark cases of breakup in the United States and United Kingdom to identify the main immediate, historical causes of the breakups. Then, against this database, we explore the conventional explana-tions of breakup and probe the extent to which they fit the facts and yield in-sight into the underlying causes. We emerge with a great deal of knowledge, but with more questions than answers about why breakup has become so important.

In Chapter 3, The Real Reason Why Breakup Creates Value, we highlight the value destruction to which the multibusiness company is vulnerable, and the way in which breakup removes value destruction. We find that there is a much better way of organizing corporations.

Chapter 4, Do You Need to Break Up?, as the title suggests, addresses this question and is written to help managers determine whether their corporation should seriously consider breaking up. It presents a methodology that we have used successfully with a substantial number of MBCs.

In Chapter 5, The Anatomy of a Breakup, we describe what the process feels like from the inside. Initially, most managers view breakup as an alien and threatening prospect. External pressure tends to be the force that initially puts breakup on the board's agenda. Breakup then becomes like any other major corporate-finance maneuver: dictated by timetables, lawyers, and financiers with that curious alternation of excitement and boredom peculiar to corporate restructurings. Finally, after the deed is done, there is usually a release of previously suppressed energy, entrepreneurial vim, and a new sense of control and self-reliance. We summarize our conclusions about how best to get through the breakup process with tips for managers.

Chapter 6, How to Profit from Breakup, provides a guide to the coming bonanza for the benefit of investors and shareholders.

Chapter 7, Breakup: The Future, provides a summary and a conclusion. It speculates on where the breakup movement will end. We ask what will happen to multibusiness companies, to head offices, to the balance between large and small corporations, and to the managers involved. We predict an inevitable evolution from the MBC to FBC or single-business company form. We explain why breakup is an act of enlightenment, not surrender.

Coda: An Appeal to Journalists, Analysts, and Management Writers. We conclude by appealing to analysts and journalists to help speed the change. We offer a series of questions for them to put to corporate managers and we list four common fallacies in management thinking. We want analysts and journalists to help us root out these fallacies and speed the improvement in management thinking that is now under way.

The Appendix describes the Breakup 100. Compiled by OC&C Strategy Consultants, this listing assesses the degree to which companies should have breakup on their agendas. It presents detailed analyses of 100 US companies and summary data on 100 UK companies. By comparing the scores of today's companies with those of historic breakups, we can judge which companies should seriously be considering breakup.

Chapter 1

The Epidemic Breaks Out

The evidence that breakups work could scarcely be clearer . . . the
average spinoff performed 25 percent better than the stock
market in the first 18 months after breakup.
—*Spin-offs,* JP Morgan

In a short time, breakup has become a major force,
growing with apparently relentless vigor.
—*Spin-offs,* JP Morgan

The breakup phenomenon is not new. The US tax rules by which spin-off transactions are structured were written in 1954. But large-scale breakups are more recent than that, only becoming significant in the 1980s. The first really big breakup occurred in 1982–83 when the US government won its antitrust suit against AT&T. AT&T had been America's largest industrial company, enjoying a monopoly of local and long-distance telephone services and of the supply of telephone equipment. Ma Bell was broken up into seven separate Baby Bells, regional local call providers, leaving AT&T with long-distance and international calls, the Bell Telephone research labs, and its telephone manufacturing business.

THE ESCALATION OF BREAKUP IN THE US

The escalating value of US breakup transactions can be seen from Figure 3. Excluding the AT&T deal, the value of breakoffs averaged only $1.1 billion each year during the period 1980–84; for 1985–89, this average jumped over five times to $6.1 billion; and for the 1990–94 period, it leapt further to an average of $14.8 billion. In 1995 we saw a tidal wave of breakoffs, with a total value of $76.7 billion, two and a half times the 1994 level (itself a previous record), and five times the average of the early 1990s. The compound annual growth rate of the value of breakoffs from 1991 to 1995 was a staggering 104 percent. Growth continued in 1996; just two breakups—that of Lucent from AT&T, and EDS from General Motors—have accounted for almost $50 billion on their own.

FIGURE 3

Dollar Value of Breakoff Transactions in the US, 1980–95

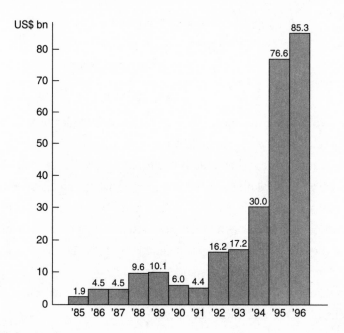

Source: IFR Securities Data

The importance of breakups can also be measured relative to the total value of all corporate divestitures. As Figure 4 shows, breakoffs only became an important method of disposal in the early 1990s. Breakoffs as a proportion of the total then grew explosively, to reach 37 percent of the total in 1995.

BRITAIN JOINS IN THE BREAKUP PHENOMENON

Breakoffs are also important on the other side of the Atlantic. Breakoffs began rather later in the UK, with two transactions in 1987 and four in 1988. They only became significant in value terms in 1989, when seven deals totaled $3.9 billion, compared with a US figure of $10.1 billion for that year. Thereafter, the value of transactions has shown no real trend (see Figure 5). The

FIGURE 4

Breakoffs in the US as a Percentage of the Value of Total Divestments, 1981–95

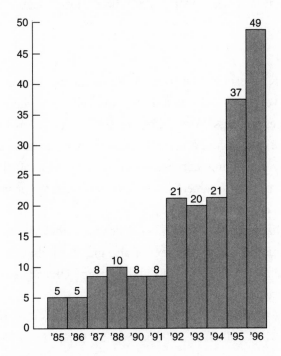

Source: IFR Securities Data

FIGURE 5

Total Dollar Value of Breakoffs in the UK, 1989–95

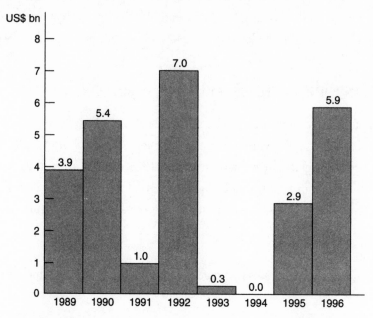

Source: IFR Securities Data

number of UK transactions has remained in single figures each year, but includes some very large individual deals, especially the demerger of Zeneca, the life sciences business, from the chemical company ICI in 1992.

You can see from Figure 6 that UK breakoffs have become an important, though highly fluctuating, component in the total value of all divestitures, ranging from less than 1 percent in 1994 to 34 percent the previous year; the average is a shade over 10 percent.

What has happened to the number of deals and their average value?

The total number of transactions has also increased, though not as fast as the value. The numbers of breakoffs in the US and UK can be seen in Figure 7, and their average value in Figure 8.

The average size of American breakup transactions has risen steadily in the 1990s, from $170 million in 1990 to over $1 billion in 1995. In the UK, there has been no trend in the average value of deals: it fluctuated from $3.5

FIGURE 6

Breakoffs in the UK as a Percentage of the Value of Total Divestments, 1989–96

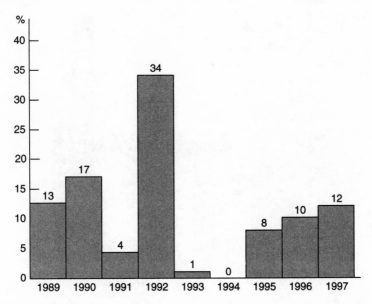

Source: IFR Securities Data

billion in 1992 (as a result of the huge ICI/Zeneca demerger) to $4 million in 1994. It is important to note, however, that in both the UK and the US, there have been very large breakups and also a number of much smaller ones. In America, transactions in excess of $500 million typically constitute only about 20 percent of total transactions, varying fairly consistently within the 10 to 30 percent band.

DO BREAKUPS WORK?

Yes! The evidence that breakups work could scarcely be clearer. In a 1995 note entitled *Spin-offs,* international investment bank JP Morgan looked at the stock-market performance of 77 spin-offs since their independence. As shown in Figure 9, the average spin-off performed 25 percent better than the stock market during the first 18 months after breakup. Tellingly, the outper-

FIGURE 7

Number of Breakoffs in the US and UK, 1980–95

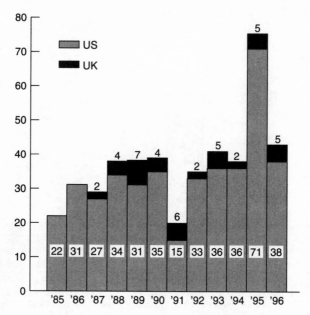

Source: IFR Securities Data

formance also increased steadily over time, so that it is probable that future research, allowing a longer period after breakup, will show significantly greater outperformance.

There is also some evidence for superior returns by parent companies after the spin-off.

JP Morgan undertook an analysis of the post-spin-off share price performance of those transactions involving at least $850 million in market value and 20 percent of the parent's pretransaction value. This subsample outperformed the market by 18 percent in the first year after the spin-off. In Morgan's words, "it appears that the remaining slimmer parent company, on average, does materially better than the market following the separation."

In other words, where the spin-off is significant, the combined entity has outperformed the market by around 20 percent.

FIGURE 8

Average Value of Breakoffs in the US and UK, 1980–95

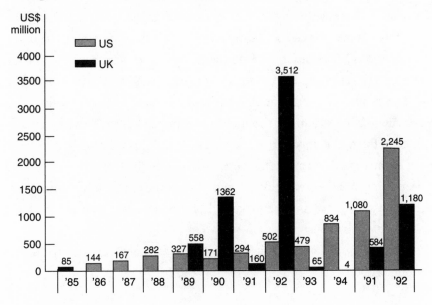

Source: IFR Securities Data

FIGURE 9

Stock Market Outperformance of US Spin-offs in the First Eighteen Months

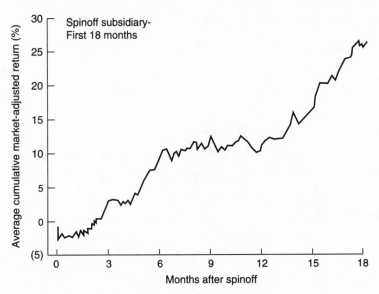

JP Morgan's study generated the even more fascinating result that smaller breakups performed still better. The study grouped the spin-offs into two segments: those with an initial market capitalization under $200 million, and those above. We can see from Figure 10 that the outperformance of the larger spin-offs was around 13 percent, but the smaller spin-offs beat the market by a staggering 45 percent and the trend was still sharply upward.

The significance of this finding has yet to sink in. If smaller breakups are actually so beneficial, there should be many more of them. If there are many more of them, the importance and value of breakups will rise even faster in the future than they have in the past. Especially in the UK, where there have been comparatively few breakups, and most of their value has been concentrated in a very small number of large deals, there is great potential for many more smaller breakups.

It should be remembered that share price movements can stretch out over a long period of time:

FIGURE 10
Stock Market Outperformance of Small versus Large US Spin-offs

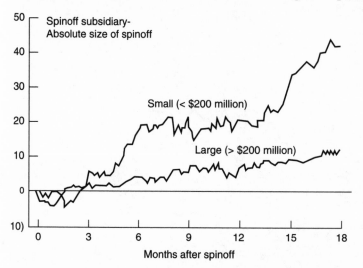

- Often there is a rumor that something is going to happen; it can be just a guess or even a suggestion by a journalist or a security analyst; if the market takes it seriously, the first price reaction occurs.
- Sometimes events that are typical precursors of a breakup can similarly cause movement in the price, especially if an active investor takes a stake in the company.
- The announcement itself typically leads to another jump in the price.
- Following the actual spin-off, more price movement generally occurs.

The data in Figures 9 and 10 refer only to price movements after the spin-off has been completed. Research into price movements before completion suggests that they double the 20 percent or so uplift that happens after completion.

BREAKUPS IN THE UNITED STATES: LANDMARK EVENTS

There have been twenty particularly significant cases in recent US history, involving seventeen companies. These are summarized in Figure 11.

Some recent highlights:

In June 1995, Rand Araskog shocks and delights Wall Street by announcing a breakup of ITT Corporation into three more focused corporations: ITT Hartford Group (insurance); ITT Industries (automotive, military, and electronics); and ITT Destinations (hotels, gambling, entertainment, and information). The breakup proposal is a huge volte-face for America's most diversified conglomerate.

Three months later, AT&T announces another three-way split (a "trivestiture"), this time into communications, communications hardware, and computers.

In 1996, General Motors announced the spin-off of EDS, its information systems subsidiary—after constant goading by its founder, the inimitable Ross Perot. Could this be the start of GM's total breakup?

Then PepsiCo announced the spin-off of its restaurant businesses, Pizza Hut, Kentucky Fried Chicken, and Taco Bell, to be run by Andy Pearson,

FIGURE 11

Twenty Landmark Breakups in the US, 1982–96

Year announced	Company	Spin-offs/ new entities	Total sales revenue ($ billion)	Number of companies after breakup	Significance
1982	AT&T	Baby Bells	59.6	8	The first mega-breakup!
1992	Baxter	Caremark	1.4	2	Classic competitive conflict
1992	Marriott	Hotel Real Estate	1.7	2	The danger of alienating debt holders
1992	Pacific Telesis	Pac/Tel Corp. (cellular communications)	1.0	2	Cellular telephones– a recurring participant in breakups
1994	Sears	Allstate Insurance	21.0	2	The biggest IPO (initial public offering)
1994	General Mills	Darden Restaurants	3.2	2	Pure focus
1994	Lilly	Guidant Medical Devices	0.9	2	Roaring stock market success
1995	ITT Corporation	ITT Hartford ITT Industries ITT Corporation (hotels)	23.6	3	The end of the conglomerate era
1995	Grace	National Medical Care	2.1	2	An alternative to trade sale
1995	Marriott	Concession business	1.2	2	Second time right
1995	AT&T	NCR & Lucent	29.5	3	Huge; incontrovertible commercial logic
1995	3M	Imation (data storage and imaging products)	2.2	2	The problem of parenting a mature business in a growth company
1995	Baxter	Allegiance	3.4	2	Long advocated and anticipated
1996	Tenneco	Newport News (shipbuilder)	1.8	2	Conglomerate unbundling
1996	General Motors	EDS (management of corporate information systems)	12.4	2	The start of the General Motors breakup?
1996	Corning	Pharmaceutical Services: Clinical Labs	2.0	3	A clustering exercise
1996	PepsiCo	Restaurant businesses	11.0	2	Focus to catch Coke
1996	American Brands	Gallaher Tobacco (UK)	7.4	2	Final exit from tobacco and its problems
1996	Monsanto	Chemicals	3.0	2	Final exit from original business
1997	Rockwell International	Automotive Components	3.1	2	Transformation to high tech

PepsiCo's former CEO. PepsiCo has clearly decided that it needs all the well-known benefits of focus if it is to catch Coca-Cola.

BREAKUPS IN THE UNITED KINGDOM: LANDMARK EVENTS

In the UK, there have been ten key breakups, and one notable near miss, when Forte unsuccessfully proposed a breakup as an alternative to the successful takeover by Granada. These are summarized in Figure 12.

FIGURE 12

Ten Landmark Breakups in the UK, 1982–96

Year announced	Company	Spin-offs/ new entities	Total sales revenue ($ billion)	Number of companies after breakup	Significance
1990	Courtaulds	Textiles	1.0	2	A UK forerunner
1990	Racal	Vodaphone (cellular telephones)	0.2	2	Another cellular telephone play
1990	BAT	Argos (catalog retailer) Wiggins Teape Appleton (paper)	2.7	3	Well executed and long overdue; defensive
1993	ICI	Zeneca (pharmaceuticals)	4.0	2	Huge value creation exercise
1994	ECC	CAMAS (construction, aggregates, materials, and services)	0.4	2	Disappointing market reaction
1995	Hanson	US Industries	2.0	2	Initially precarious owing to heavy indebtedness
1995	Thorn EMI	Thorn rentals	1.5	2	The culmination of a ten year unbundling sale
1996	Hanson	Hanson Industries The Energy Group Millenium Chemicals Imperial Tobacco	9.1	4	Very disappointing market reaction due to lack of fundamental value destruction and creation of further MBCs
1996	British Gas	Centrica (domestic trading and supply)	8.0	2	A delayed deal with dubious rationale
1996	Lonrho	Hotel business	1.7	2	Dissolution of MBC with no value added after retirement of founder

Whereas the pace of breaking up in the UK has been more intermittent, there appears to be a resurgence in interest. In recent months, allied Domecq, Pearson, and BAT have all been the subject of rumor and conjecture about possible breakup.

PARALLELS WITH OTHER CORPORATE RESTRUCTURINGS

The scale of breakups may now be compared to other major corporate restructuring initiatives. Figure 13 compares the total value of breakoffs to the total value of Leveraged Buyouts (LBOs) in the United States.

The enormous rise of LBOs in the 1980s was widely attributed to the availability of so-called junk bonds. The market for these securities began to dry up in the middle of the decade and the prevalence of LBOs diminished rapidly thereafter. After a peak in 1988, the market all but disappeared within two years. The transaction value of breakoffs, which was climbing throughout this period, passed that of LBOs in 1992. It seems likely that the 1997 total for breakoffs will exceed the 1988 peak for LBOs.

FIGURE 13

The Value of Breakoffs and Leveraged Buyouts (LBOs) in the US, 1982–95

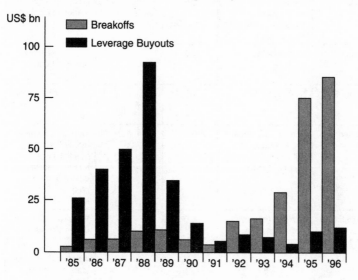

WHY IS THIS HAPPENING?

In a short period of time, breakup has become a major force, growing with apparently relentless vigor. In terms of absolute size, breakups on both sides of the Atlantic have suddenly become a key component of corporate change. But why? Is breakup just a financial engineering fad? Or are there sound reasons why it will continue growing? What does it tell us about the state of big business? We answer these questions in Chapters 2 and 3.

Chapter 2

What Drives Breakup?

Management explanations of the reasons for breaking up tell us only
something of the whys; they do not explain the dramatic
increases in value we have observed.

Focus is a slippery concept. When are you focused enough? Can
you have too much focus? How do we define it?

Perhaps breakup has no economic logic to explain why it is growing
so fast . . . we do not believe this . . . there is more
to breakup than has met the eye.

W hat is behind the breakup phenomenon? Is it just a series of special reasons specific to each corporation that has decided to take
the plunge? Or are there some basic, common forces at work? What are the
underlying reasons for breakups, and how do they create value? These are
the questions tackled in Chapters 2 and 3.

In the first section following our examination of landmark breakups, we
analyze the reasons cited for these moves by executives and commentators.
We ask to what extent the breakups were spontaneous moves and to what

37

extent they were a response to outside pressure, and we attempt to categorize and summarize the ostensible reasons. In the second section, we look at the reasons advanced for the breakup movement as a whole. Although all the explanations offered have some truth and insight, we are not satisfied that any are deep enough to tell the whole story or explain why breakups create so much value.

Chapter 3 puts forward the real reasons for breakup and the revolutionary implications for how we organize our corporations.

INFERENCES FROM LANDMARK BREAKUP CASES

In Chapter 1, we introduced thirty landmark breakup cases from the United States and the United Kingdom. We have looked at available published materials and conducted an extensive interview program with contemporary observers, commentators, and, most valuably, the participants themselves. We conducted comprehensive face-to-face and telephone interviews and reviewed a mountain of press and journal comment and analysis on the breakup phenomenon before arriving at our judgments.

In each case of breakup we have looked at the presence or absence and relative importance of the following immediate causes.

Managers' genuine desire for increased focus. There is a powerful body of evidence that corporations focusing on one business, or on a small number, tend to perform better than corporations in a wide variety of different businesses. How far were the executives leading breakups influenced by the desire to simplify and focus their corporations?

Management's desire to see a "fair" share price. Sometimes management and shareholders believe that breakup is necessary to obtain a "fair" valuation of their corporation. Stock market analysts tend to prefer a "pure play" to a company that is in two or more broadly defined industries. Was this motivation apparent in our cases? Was the corporation lagging its comparable stock market peer group in the period before breakup?

Finding money to reduce debt. Did the parent organization see the spin-off as a way to get its hands on a lot of cash?

Fear of takeover. Was the corporation subject to breakup typically mentioned beforehand as a candidate for hostile takeover? Is it possible that breakup was initially seen as a less unpalatable alternative to takeover, and adopted on this basis?

Competitive conflict. Was there a built-in conflict of interest among the company's divisions? Were customers balking at doing business with the sister division of a competitor?

Poor performance. Has the company finally given up on one of its businesses, one that it tried for years to bring up to a "normal" level of financial performance?

Pressure from regulatory and antitrust authorities. Was the breakup either forced by antitrust action or designed to avoid it? Was the industry regulator making it impossible to make profits?

Quarantining a problem. Is there a problem business whose total exposure could threaten the company?

Better tax efficiency of breakup compared to trade sale. In most cases, the US and UK tax authorities allow spin-offs and demergers to occur without either shareholders or the companies involved incurring income or capital-gains tax liability. Shareholders receive two or more pieces of paper in exchange for the previous one, but nothing else changes. If, instead of breakup, a business is sold by a corporation, the latter will normally be taxed on any capital gain. How far did considerations of tax efficiency appear to be pivotal?

Financial engineering fad. Fashion can be a major determinant of corporate behavior. Moreover, like all financial engineering moves, breakup can be highly lucrative for advisers. Is there evidence that managers undertaking each of these breakups were influenced by a bandwagon mentality or pushed into the move by their advisers?

Figures 14 and 15 detail the apparent causes, from among those itemized above, of the breakup in each of our thirty landmark cases in the US and in the UK. We also suggest the additional reasons that were not formally put forward in the official reasons at the time of the announcement.

What are we to make of these explanations? Do they tell the whole story? Figure 16 lists the relative importance of the immediate causes, as reflected in our sample.

While the results are informative, they represent subjective judgments, and it is important not to interpret them too mechanistically. Fear of takeover and share price underperformance appear to have been important in many cases, yet neither of these causes can be viewed as a complete or totally satisfactory explanation of breakup. Both beg these two questions: Why was there fear of takeover and poor share performance? And why was breakup felt to be a suitable remedy?

To answer these questions, we need to probe each explanation carefully.

Conventional Explanations of Breakup Tested

Not surprisingly, the explosion of breakups on both sides of the Atlantic has attracted a great deal of attention from journalists, academics, stockbrokers' analysts, and investment bankers. In this section we look at the various explanations advanced for breakups and draw what insight we can from them. But we also point out that each explanation, and even a mix of all of them, is inadequate and incomplete. While they can help to explain individual breakups, they do not explain why there's money on the table in the first place. Why is value released when corporations are broken up? Why are they worth more dead than alive? We will return to these questions later in Chapter 4.

MANAGERS' GENUINE DESIRE FOR INCREASED FOCUS

Almost every company undertaking breakup offers the justification of focus. Documents regularly use phrases such as "these actions will afford management the opportunity to concentrate its efforts on its core widget business."

FIGURE 14

Twenty Landmark US Breakups: Main Immediate Causes

Year announced	Company	New entities	Reasons stated	Additional reasons
1982	AT&T	Baby Bells	Regulatory (anti-trust)	
1995	AT&T	NCR and Lucent	Focus Competitive conflict	Reduce debt Poor performer
1992	Baxter International	Caremark (home health care)	Competitive conflict	
1995	Baxter International	Allegiance (hospital distribution)	Focus Fair value	Competitive conflict
1994	General Mills	Darden Restaurants	Focus	
1996	General Motors	EDS	Focus	Competitive conflict
1995	Grace	National Medical Care	Focus Fair value Reduce debt	
1995	ITT Corporation	ITT Hartford ITT Industries ITT Corporation (hotels)	Focus Enhance capital raising	Fair value
1994	Lilly	Guidant (medical devices)	Focus Fair value	
1992	Marriott	Hotel real estate	Focus	Reduce debt Quarantine problem
1995	Marriott	Concession business	Focus Enhance capital raising	
1995	3M	Imation	Poor performer	
1992	Pacific Telesis	Cellular	Regulatory Fair value	
1994	Sears	Allstate Insurance	Focus	Reduce debt
1996	Tenneco	Newport News (shipbuilder)	Focus	Reduce debt
1996	PepsiCo	Restaurant businesses	Focus Poor performer	Reduce debt
1996	American Brands	Gallaher Tobacco (UK)	Fair value Poor performer	Quarantine problem
1996	Monsanto	Chemicals	Fair value Poor performer	
1996	Rockwell International	Automotive components	Focus	Fair value

FIGURE 15

Ten Landmark UK Breakups: Main Immediate Causes

Year announced	Company	New entities	Reasons stated	Additional reasons
1990	BAT	Argus (catalog retailer), Arjo Wiggins (paper)	Focus	Takeover fear
1996	British Gas	British Gas Centrica	Focus	Quarantine problem
1990	Courtaulds	Chemicals, Coatings	Focus	Takeover fear
1994	ECC	Aggregates	Focus	
1995	Hanson	US Industries	Focus	Reduce debt
1996	Hanson	Breakup	Focus	
1993	ICI	Zeneca	Focus, Fair value	Takeover fear Enhance capital raising
1996	Lonrho	Hotel business	Focus, Fair value	
1990	Racal	Vodaphone	Focus	Takeover fear
1995	Thorn EMI	EMI Music, Thorn rentals	Focus, Fair value	

FIGURE 16

Relative Importance of Immediate Causes of Breakup in the Landmark Cases

Rank	Reason	Number of occurences			Comment
		US	UK	Total	
1	Focus	12	10	22	The standard answer
2	Fair value	7	3	10	Everything to do with the stock price
3	Reduce debt	7	1	8	Little noted by commentators
5	Fear of takeover	0	4	4	Mainly UK
5	Competitive conflict	4	0	4	Unwinding vertical integration
4	Poor performer	5	0	5	
7	Regulatory	2	0	2	Telecoms
6	Enhance capital raising	2	1	3	
6	Quarantine problem	2	1	3	
8	Tax efficiency	1	0	1	Relative to sale
–	Financial Engineering	0	0	0	
		42	20	62	

Sometimes this is a smokescreen for other rationales that may prove embarrassing to admit.

But it also evinces a genuine desire on the part of those running corporations to focus, as far as possible, on just one line of business.

The investment community certainly believes that focus is good and that a lack of it is bad. In a 1996 paper, *European Spin-offs,* JP Morgan observes that:

> *Under-valuation usually arises when a company is viewed as too diversified . . . for several reasons:*
>
> *more overhead is needed to manage a diverse portfolio*
>
> *highly profitable businesses may subsidize dogs*
>
> *management may pay too much for diversifying acquisitions where investors could buy them directly without paying a control premium*
>
> *investors do not have the opportunity to invest directly in a business they want to be involved in*
>
> *diversification makes it difficult to analyze them*
>
> *analysts' coverage is often restricted to the company's primary business activity and the rest is overlooked or covered poorly.*

When Pacific Telesis, the California telephone corporation, spun off Air Touch, its cellular telephone company, Sam Ginn stepped down from being CEO to the same position at Air Touch. He found the apparent demotion fulfilling: "I can tell you as CEO [of Air Touch] that I know a hell of a lot more about this business now than I did when I was at Telesis, managing 65,000 people and running 20 lines of business."

In May 1995, General Mills, one of America's leading cereal and food companies, announced that it would spin off Darden Restaurants, an operation accounting for about 40 percent of General Mills total revenues.

Previously, attempts had been made to cross-train its senior executives. Joe Lee, one of the best restaurateurs in the US, was running the grocery business; his opposite number from groceries was running restaurants. In explaining the breakup, Steve Sanger, the new chairman and CEO of General Mills, was quoted in the *Minneapolis Star Tribune:* "What it's all about is management focus . . . that's what this split is about. . . . What you've got now is most everyone playing to their forehand."

The executives of the newly independent restaurant company are reported to be enthusiastic about their stock options, which are now tied solely to their own performance. The element of focus on compensation is repeated again and again.

At Eli Lilly, the spin-off of Guidant has been a clear success. Charles Schalliol, Executive Director of Corporate Finance and Investment Banking, told us: "Guidant has been a win-win proposition. Greater strategic focus, better alignment of incentives and market discipline. Guidant went public at 14½; it's now trading around 50."

It seems obvious that when managers concentrate on what they know best, they do better; and that even the most talented managers can come unstuck when they venture into areas they do not understand, or where their deeply held beliefs and responses, built up and reinforced by success in the original business, are not appropriate. It is also logical that a corporation can be more single-minded about its dedication to customers and its wish to beat competitors if it is in a few lines of business, or, ideally, just one.

Indeed, we will argue in the coming chapters that any multibusiness company (MBC), to be effective, must really focus. But we have a specific way of thinking about focus, which is explained in more detail in Chapter 4.

And yet, there are certain problems with focus as the main explanation for breakups. One problem lies in the very plausibility and credibility of the focus explanation. Because it is a fashionable and "politically correct" nostrum, we suspect that it is deployed rather more prominently, and even sometimes more glibly, than its considerable merits deserve. Focus is certainly a more pleasing and tactful benefit to highlight than the desire to escape from share price underperformance, the threat of a hostile bid, or the need to quarantine a potentially horrendous corporate liability.

For example, British Gas has recently announced a breakup to separate a new company, Centrica, which will be responsible for domestic trading and supply. The parent, after a change of mind, will now retain the name, British Gas. In explaining the move in *The Sunday Times* (of London), the chairman,

Richard Giordano, noted the need for greater focus: "British Gas was like a fire station . . . the bell would ring and all the talented managers would rush off to solve the problem."

This is not a wholly convincing explanation. Breaking into two pieces is not a sufficient remedy for the kind of managerial behavior described by Mr. Giordano. Moreover, in the case of British Gas, there is a particularly powerful reason for the breakup that has nothing to do with the merits of focus. Currently, British Gas is under an obligation to take gas from the North Sea at around twice the current price, and, unless the obligation can be renegotiated, it could have devastating financial consequences. Paul Spedding, an analyst at Kleinwort Benson, commented in *The Sunday Times* (of London) that: "The best description of British Gas Energy is that it is an option on solving the contractual renegotiation."

Another difficulty with focus is that it is an elastic concept, especially linked to the dubious concept of "core businesses." Statements of what constitute core businesses are often worded to stretch conveniently over most of the existing portfolio. In a breakup, the original management team is often left to oversee around half of the previous portfolio, with the comments that it can now focus on the company's "core businesses." But the term "core" may only provide an after-the-fact description of what has happened, not a criterion for action. Management may be saying no more than, "these are the businesses we have decided to keep." If so, the notion of core businesses offers little insight into why the need for breakup arose. In many cases, breakups have been far less radical than they could have been, leaving more than one line of business, and in some cases a large number, within each new entity. When is more focus enough? If greater focus is good, when and where should you stop? Does there come a point at which focus ceases to have benefits, or actually leads to no benefits? If not, is it good enough to have "more focus" when you could have had "even more focus"?

And how should we define focus? There is no commonly accepted definition, among either academics or business people. Notions of business-relatedness and synergy vie with SIC codes and linguistic labels to determine what is close enough and what is too far away. If you make financial software for personal computers, and also have a games-software business, a financial services company, and a computer-facilities management company, are you focused or ripe for a breakup? And if the latter, should you split into two, three, or four parts?

Later, we will provide our answers to the focus question. We will argue that focus is not just a matter of narrowing the scope of the portfolio so that it can be described in fewer words. The key to focus is the existence of a matchup between the needs of the portfolio businesses and specific skills at the center which can be of help to the businesses. Without such a fit between needs and capabilities, focus is just another cling-film concept.

Our overall verdict on focus is that of all the explanations examined, it comes closest to highlighting the real economic advantages of breakup. It is clear that breakups create value; focus is part of the reason why. But it is, at best, only half the truth.

GETTING A FAIR SHARE PRICE

Eleven out of our thirty landmark cases cited the desire to raise the company's share price as one of the main causes of breakup. In ten out of the eleven cases this was publicly announced or emphasized by our interviewees, who used phrases like "fair value," and the desire to induce the stock market to value a corporation "correctly."

Increasingly, executive bonuses and options are directly tied to rising shareholder value. When investment bankers are asked how to raise the share price, they often look at a disparate portfolio and say "break it up." This appears to work. In their comprehensive academic study of spin-offs over a number of years, Cusatis, Miles, and Woolridge conclude that "we observe superior long-term investment performance for spin-offs. In contrast to the similar and more common newly traded security, the IPO spin-offs provide positive abnormal returns over an extended period. Surprisingly we find that parent firms also offer superior post-spin-off long-term investment performance." (P. Cusatis, J.A. Miles, and J.R. Woolridge, "Restructuring

Through Spin-offs: The Stock Market Evidence," *Journal of Financial Economics,* 1993)

This 1993 study was corroborated and reinforced by the JP Morgan research, which we summarized in Chapter 1 (see Figures 9 and 10). So if breakups are often motivated by the desire to raise the share price, one can understand why. Yet this still does not answer the question of why breakups raise the stock price.

Here, there are two competing "explanations." One, often advanced by CEOs and chairmen who have undertaken breakups, is that somehow the market got it wrong before the event and breakup enabled a correct valuation. We do not find this convincing. The other standard explanation comes from academics, investment analysts, and stockbrokers, who stress that the stock market prefers "pure plays." This explanation is fine as far as it goes, but begs the real question—*why?* Let's examine each explanation in turn.

Management's idea that a higher and more "fair" stock price can result from breakup comes in two forms: wanting credit for a go-go company whose prospects are not reflected in the share price; or getting rid of a conglomerate discount by presenting separate businesses as more focused entities, in which management can concentrate on fewer things (and do them better).

Racal's experience with Vodafone is an example of the go-go rationale. Sir Ernest Harrison, the astute and value-oriented chairman of Britain's Racal plc, experienced continued frustration at the way the market failed to reflect the huge potential of its cellular telephone subsidiary. After floating half of its stock to the public on a very high market valuation, Vodafone's stock price began to slip back and Racal's fell again toward its original level. Not only did Vodafone's rating fail to match that of other cellular telephone operators, the entire market capitalization of the Racal group was less than the value of its 80 percent stake in Vodafone, worth nearly £3 billion, at £2.9 billion. Management frustration with this situation was reflected in the 1991 annual report which noted: ". . . The Board commenced a detailed review of how this situation could be rectified. A full demerger of Racal Telecom and, in due course, of the security group, appeared a practicable solution."

On completion of the breakup, Vodafone's market value skyrocketed, tripling the growth rate of the All Share Index over the next seventeen months. By September 1996, its market capitalization had reached £7.1 billion, versus £3.5 billion at the time of the demerger. The market was simply saying that Vodafone was worth less as long as Racal was running it. When it was spun off in its entirety, its rating rapidly moved up to that of its cellular telephone rivals.

But whereas Sir Ernest Harrison and his colleagues see this as evidence that a breakup was needed to allow a "correct" valuation of Racal's businesses, we draw a different inference. The market's reaction to the initial carveout of Vodafone was clear and protracted: it was not impressed. It was not until the new business was removed from the control of the parent organization that a sustainable increase in the share price occurred. To us, the message is unambiguous. It was the negative influence of the Racal head office that the market was discounting. While management believes that the stock market got it wrong until the breakup, an alternative explanation is that the market got it right throughout. Vodafone's value was being seriously reduced under Racal.

It is worth belaboring this vital point a little more. As a shareholder in Racal, the dividends you would get from Vodafone would pass through Racal. The market was valuing this stream of dividends significantly lower than the dividends going directly to shareholders from Vodafone. In other words, the market expected Harrison's team to misuse part of these dividends—not in any illegal way, but through poor investment decisions.

Moreover, the whole of Vodafone was undervalued compared to its peers. The market was predicting that Vodafone would underperform its peer group while it was majority-owned by Racal. The market felt that Racal's influence on Vodafone would be negative and was attributing more than £1 billion of value destruction to Racal's influence. Once its influence was removed, the stock bounced up to the level of its peers.

Removing the conglomerate discount is the other variant of the "fair-price" explanation of breakup. In this case, managers leading conglomerates believe that they suffer an unreasonable penalty because the stock market, irrationally, dislikes conglomerates. Breakup is therefore necessary to obtain a "fair" valuation.

That the conglomerate discount exists is undeniable. Conglomerates in both the US and the UK currently trade on Price/Earnings ratios ("P/Es") substantially below those of comparable businesses. What is at issue is whether or not this discount is deserved.

There have been few complete breakups of conglomerates (although many limited spin-offs). The three cases that are most relevant are the 1995 breakup of ITT into three parts, described in the Introduction; and two British cases, the partial breakup of BAT Industries in 1986, and the announcement in 1996 of Hanson's breakup into four parts.

Did breakup remove the conglomerate discount in these cases? The evidence from this very small sample is mixed. In the case of ITT, the share price soon went up by 30 percent. For BAT, the breakups both added extra value and have continued to outperform the market. Yet BAT itself, which remains a diversified mixture of tobacco and financial services, still has a P/E in single figures. It still suffers a "conglomerate" (and tobacco) discount. In the case of Hanson, after a brief bump, the share price actually fell as a result of the announcement.

We believe that the stock market behaves rationally with regard to conglomerates. These three cases are no exception. The increase in ITT's share price can be explained by the extra value attributed to the insurance and leisure businesses as stand-alone entities, freed from ITT's clutches. Conversely, the low valuation of BAT's residual mix of tobacco and financial services suggests that the group, despite its world-class performance in tobacco, subtracts value from the financial services business. As for Hanson, three of the four pieces after the breakup are still themselves conglomerates, so there is no reason to value them more highly. A part of the fall in the share price can also be attributed to a lower aggregate dividend from the new companies compared to the integrated Hanson and to the unwinding of a well-designed tax structure.

Academics, brokers, and corporate financiers advance a convincing explanation for the generally favorable stockmarket response to breakups: the concept of the "pure play." An oil company that has no nonoil interests is a "pure play" (and if it did nothing but oil exploration it would be an even purer play). An oil company that owns a chemical or a minerals company is a "mixed play." The stock market, it is said, prefers pure plays.

In another 1996 paper, *Corporate Clarity,* analysts at JP Morgan explain that "The market rewards corporate clarity. Over the 24 months following a major business shift, clarifying firms outperformed the market by 14.6 percent and outperformed diversifying firms by 19.1 percent."

Companies are quoted under different sectors in much of the world's financial press. Since stock-market analysts specialize by sector, they have a poorer understanding of the businesses outside their sectors. Hence the complaint that diversified corporations are "almost impossible to follow" because they defy sector classification.

When breakups occur, there is an increase in the number of analysts following the businesses. For example, one month before spinning off its brokerage subsidiary, Dean Witter, the diversified retail and financial services group, Sears, was followed by twenty-one analysts. By 1996 after the breakup, thirty-one analysts were covering Sears, fifteen were following Dean Witter, and another twenty-six were writing about the insurance spin-off, Allstate, giving a total of seventy-two analysts. This increase in interest ought to help the share price of Sears and its spin-offs.

So the pure play explanation has logic to it. Yet it is inherently implausible as a full explanation. It assumes that analysts and fund managers are so limited in their quantitative skills that they cannot effectively value a multisector company. It also assumes that multisector corporations are systematically undervalued, and that the financial community has not realized this and gone on to benefit from the higher dividend yield on offer. If even one person had this insight, he or she could make superior gains by investing in such companies. These assumptions are clearly unreasonable, casting doubt on the explanation.

It is true that analysts and institutions like pure plays. But it is unlikely that they consistently undervalue mixed plays by large amounts. It is true that when mixed plays turn into pure plays, the share price tends to go up.

But this is not because an arbitrary valuation anomaly has been corrected. A more reasonable explanation is that, in the process, real value has been created and is being reflected in the higher stock price. We conclude, therefore, that although the pure play explanation can point us in the right direction, it cannot deliver the explanation we are seeking.

Incidentally, it is interesting that our discussions with management did not identify a single case where the architects of breakup cited the wish to create pure plays as their motivation. In fact, CEOs and chairmen sometimes see the creation of pure plays as one of the drawbacks of a breakup, since a pure play is more likely to attract a bid. Although a bid is good for the shareholders, it is bad for incumbent management. For instance, Colin Southgate of Thorn EMI very frankly told us:

> The one thing I have really worried about [in the breakup of Thorn from EMI] is EMI. It's a national asset. It has given great pleasure to people for a hundred years. I don't want somebody coming after it right after this deal.

The increased potential for attracting an acquisition is clearly a plausible explanation for the higher stock prices enjoyed by "purer play" spin-offs. The academic research cited earlier demonstrates that spun-off companies are considerably more likely to be acquired than are the average of all companies. Spin-offs tend to be single segment businesses, which have the potential to attract trade acquirers with an eye on synergy and cost saving rationalization. Such buyers are often discouraged from bidding for a portfolio of businesses because of the uncertainties involved in businesses unfamiliar to them. Spinning off the desired business presents them with a buying opportunity. Such acquisitions often occur at substantial premiums to the market price.

But even this explanation cannot conceivably account for the very large stock price runups we see in spin-off situations. More often than not, the acquisition does not occur anyway. In addition, the stock price increase applies to the whole enterprise—parent and spin-off alike, not just the acquired business.

To summarize: management's explanation that breakup is a remedy for correcting a "wrong" share price is clearly one of the reasons why many agree to a breakup. But it is not cause and effect.

The pure plays explanation is consistent with the facts. But it leaves unanswered two important questions: Why are two pieces better than one? Why are smaller pieces better? We need a deeper explanation.

GETTING MONEY TO REDUCE DEBT

Debt reduction was the third most popular explanation of breakup. In our survey of thirty landmark cases, it was an important ingredient in eight of them. As one chief executive famously said to us, "I can't feed all the tigers."

Debt reduction from a breakup can come about in two ways: 20 percent of the subsidiary is floated, the proceeds going to the original company, then the 80 percent is given as a dividend to the shareholders (this is called a "carveout"); or the subsidiary is geared up, and cash passed to the original company, then the subsidiary is spun off with the debt.

Hanson's decision to spin off US Industries in 1994 was largely driven by the need to reduce Hanson's debt; $1.4 billion of Hanson's debt was shifted to US Industries before the spin-off. The breakup of Sears Roebuck in 1994 was partly due to the requirement to reduce its $52 billion debt mountain. Debt reduction was also one of the spurs to breakup in AT&T's three-way 1995 split, in Grace's spin-off of National Medical Care the same year, in Marriott's 1992 split between hotel real estate and hotel operations, and in Tenneco's spin-off of its shipbuilding business in 1996. In all six cases, the main explanation offered publicly was the desire to provide more focus to the businesses.

Breakup is an effective way to cope with too much debt. But debt reduction is an explanation of the motive; it does not explain the value that is released. If debt reduction was the only benefit of these breakups, we might expect share values to decline (by the transaction costs), not increase. The cause of the 20 to 40 percent increase in value that results from breakup must lie elsewhere.

FEAR OF TAKEOVER

Management's fear of a hostile takeover was almost certainly an important cause of breakup in four of the ten UK landmark cases.

ICI had for many years insisted there were major technology synergies that justified keeping its chemical and pharmaceutical operations under common ownership. For years, brokers calculated that the pro forma market value of the drug business was close to, and sometimes higher than, the market capitalization of ICI as a whole. Nothing happened. In May 1991, Hanson bought a 2.8 percent stake in the company. For several months, it seemed possible that Hanson would launch a bid. ICI went on to full (and very expensive) bid alert. As Trevor Harrison, then ICI's general manager of planning, noted: "The episode underlined for ICI directors the urgent need to raise shareholder value."

When Zeneca, the biosciences company, was spun off, ICI insisted that the project had been in the planning stages for more than a year. But, clearly, Hanson had forced the issue. The combined value of ICI and Zeneca was considerably greater than before; ICI went from underperforming the stock market to outperforming. And Zeneca has consistently beaten the market since being freed to go its own way.

BAT Industries is another interesting British example. One of the world's five major cigarette companies, BAT has been hugely successful in expanding markets and in generating massive cash flow from a business whose obituary has been written many times. Like all tobacco concerns, it has diversified. Although overall performance has been good, many of its acquisitions were felt to be unnecessary diversifications.

In 1986, a trio of raiders launched a takeover bid as a prelude to breaking up the company. During the bid, BAT's management began a frantic series of spin-offs and disposals. Out went a broad spread of retailing businesses, a paper company, and a number of other miscellaneous positions. The partial breakup was sufficient to see off the bid. The spun-off businesses prospered, and their share prices as independent companies rocketed ahead.

Today BAT is in just two sectors—financial services and tobacco—and still there are calls to break up. Financial commentators are not convinced that these two businesses are suitable bedfellows.

We told the story of Forte in our introduction. As with BAT, Forte proposed a breakup after the launch of Granada's hostile bid. Unlike the case of BAT, the tactic did not work: it seemed too much like a deathbed repentance, and investors preferred Gerry Robinson. For the Forte family and management, the bid and even their own breakup proposals were traumatic. Keith Hamill, Forte's finance director at the time, said it was like "being on the Titanic when the iceberg struck." He told his staff: "Our company is going down. However, I am proud to report that it has gone down with every gun blazing."

Fear of takeover is another clear motive for breakup. It can be an excellent defense, because it releases value. Fear of takeover is not a complete explanation. It is only a proximate cause. It explains management motivation. It does not explain why value is created. The hostile acquirer is normally attracted by underperformance. If breakup is an effective defense, then shareholders must believe that breakup will eliminate the cause of underperformance.

RESOLVING A COMPETITIVE CONFLICT

The only commercially important rationale for breakup in our survey of thirty landmark case histories was the resolution of a competitive conflict. This consideration applied in four US cases.

Vertical integration is a classic expansionist maneuver, but it can backfire. This happens when the customers of one division also experience competition from another division of the same company. They may threaten to retaliate by taking their business elsewhere. Our four cases all revealed the need to unwind the vertical integration to avoid this threat.

AT&T's 1995 three-way breakup is a good example. As telecoms markets were opened up to greater competition, AT&T's vertical integration—the fact that it still made telephone equipment as well as providing telephone services—became a problem. International customers balked at the idea of buying their telephone equipment from a company competing directly with them in their home markets. The Baby Bells, fearing the prospect of AT&T's emergence as a local competitor, also became reluctant to buy AT&T equipment.

At the press conference to announce the split, the company's statement ran:

> Bob Allen and AT&T's Board Directors have concluded that on a global basis, the benefits of integration are now outweighed by the benefits of separation. It became clear that the advantages of AT&T's size and scope and vertical integration were starting to be offset by the amount of resources needed to manage the growing strategic conflicts between the services and equipment businesses that were limiting the equipment business's opportunities for growth in the marketplace.

Although Baxter International, the healthcare company, was much more successful than AT&T, it experienced a similar problem. In the early 1980s, Baxter had embarked upon a major program of vertical integration, acquiring American Hospital Supply Inc., the nation's largest supplier of hospital equipment and disposable products. The idea was that owning the largest distributor of supplies to hospitals would guarantee the success of the company's various medical product businesses.

It also decided to establish a substantial presence in alternate-site healthcare—such as walk-in surgery centers—as another in-house outlet for its products. This operation was known as Caremark International.

In 1992, Baxter announced that Caremark was no longer critical to the company's operations and spun it off to shareholders. The real reason was that the alternate-site businesses within Caremark were seen by Baxter's core hospital customers to be offering unwelcome competition. Caremark accounted for some 15 percent of Baxter's total sales and the spin-off was thus a substantial one.

But there was another vertical integration issue remaining. Baxter's distribution side offered the products of most manufacturers but was thought to give preference to the products manufactured in sister divisions. As a consequence, there was a conflict in the eyes of both customers and rival producers of relevant products. These manufacturers had sometimes shied away from using Baxter's distribution network, fearing that Baxter's sales people might push Baxter's own products more strongly than their own.

In October 1995, Baxter announced is plans to spin off the distribution business, together with a modest portfolio of products in the surgical area. Stock market reaction has been favorable.

Baxter's public announcements have not highlighted the vertical integration issue. Instead, they have stressed "focus" and "fair value" as the main motivations for the breakup. But it is clear from our investigations that the distribution and health cost management business (now called Allegiance) had negative synergy with the rest of Baxter, principally because of the competitive conflict. The *Wall Street Journal*'s report was not far off the mark:

> Baxter International Inc. says that it plans to shrink in half by spinning off its lackluster US hospital-supply business, largely undoing Baxter's decade old merger with American Hospital Supply Corp. That marriage of two health-care giants has been a stormy one, troubled by clashing cultures and numerous repeated restructuring undertaken to make the companies fit together efficiently. The hospital business has turned in some disappointing results.

A competitive conflict can be a complete explanation. It provides the motive for management to want to break up. It also explains why value is created as a result of breakup. It may be the only explanation needed for situations like Baxter's Caremark and American Hospital Supply spin-offs. Even in cases like Baxter's, however, there are other forces at work.

GETTING RID OF A POOR PERFORMER

All other causes of breakup are less significant. In five of our thirty cases, the motivation included being able to remove a poor performer. AT&T's ownership of NCR was disastrous, and the three-way breakup announced in 1995 provided the opportunity to end it gracefully.

The spin-off of 3M's Imation in 1995–96 is a similar story. The imaging and data storage business is being spun off to shareholders because it is not very profitable. Industry analysts applauded the move as a signal of 3M's intent to stay out of businesses with low margins and intense foreign competition.

Corning decided to spin off its clinical laboratory business for the same reason. After a substantial effort to reap the fruits of industry leadership, Corning management concluded that the pressures in the clinical testing business were simply too great for the business to achieve attractive returns and to grow. As James Flaws of Corning commented:

> This used to be a highly profitable and growing business and isn't anymore. Our strategic conclusion was that this business would continue to provide less profit than our company targets require and that, in any case, the growth we expect from our businesses would not be there. We say to our investors that we are a growth company. This business no longer fits that profile.

As with many of the other causes, dumping a poor performer may explain management's motivation. But it does not explain the value that is released. There is no a priori reason why stock in a company with a poor performing unit should be worth less than two stocks, one of the poor performer and one of the rest of the company. In fact, we might expect value to decline by the amount of the transaction cost. Value can only increase if one or both of the two companies performs better after the breakup. We need to understand why this might be so.

REGULATORY REASONS

In two telecoms cases—AT&T in 1982, when the company was forced to give birth to the "Baby Bells," and Pacific Telesis' 1992-93 spin-off of its cellular-phone business—the regulators' actions were decisive. Anti-trust considerations were also of some importance in Corning's spin-off of the clinical laboratory business.

In these situations we should, in theory, expect stock values to fall, because the regulator is preventing combinations that management would prefer. Where stock prices rise as a result of regulator interference, we need to understand why.

QUARANTINING A PROBLEM

We came across three cases where quarantining a potential corporate liability was an important cause of breakup.

We referred above to the case of British Gas, the UK's largest public utility. British Gas decided to break itself into two, partly at least to insulate the base distribution business from the commercial problems of Centrica, which has an obligation to buy North Sea gas at above the current market price.

Likewise, Marriott Corporation's split into a hotel-owning business (Host Marriott) and a hotel-operating business (Marriott International) was at least partly motivated by the desire to isolate the latter from the debt that Marriott had built up.

Companies that own cigarette businesses in the US are also considering breakup. Management and shareholders are concerned that litigation against cigarette companies could damage the whole organization. At a minimum, they are moving to isolate the legal responsibility.

Quarantining a problem is, therefore, a complete reason for breakup. Like many others, however, it should not result in value increases. The problem is still owned by the shareholders. To explain substantial increases in value we need to look further.

TAX EFFICIENCY COMPARED TO A DISPOSAL

"Bluntly, the number one reason companies spin off divisions rather than sell them is to avoid paying taxes," concluded Sharon Kahn in the February 1996 edition of *Global Finance*. She quoted Steven Wolitzer, managing director of Lehman Brothers: "Paying substantial taxes on a $1 billion transaction may not be as efficient as giving shareholders $1 billion worth of a company tax free."

Provided it can be proven that there is a valid business purpose, and that the distribution of shares in a breakup is not a device to distribute profits in lieu of an ordinary dividend to shareholders, the breakup can proceed tax free in both the US and the UK. In the US, three-quarters of spin-off proposals pass this test and obtain IRS approval.

Every company contemplating a breakup examines all its options. A spin-off is often the most tax effective way to do it. But no one breaks up a company to save tax.

FINANCIAL ENGINEERING FAD

Are breakups becoming a bandwagon? In our view, because they are lucrative for corporate financiers and other advisers, and because of their positive effect on stock-market performance, the whole process is in danger of turning into a self-perpetuating fad. Baxter's John Gaither said:

> There is a general expectation of share movement from a spin-off and from portfolio rearrangements. It's just the inevitable result these days of a spin-off. Everybody expects your share price to go up. One broker says that it's the best investment strategy there is, buying breakup candidates. In other words, there is a herd mentality in this thing. This does not mean that a spin-off will not add value. Some will; some will not.

With some individuals, it can even, apparently, become habit-forming. The *Wall Street Journal* commented on one activist:

> Mr. Batts [Chairman of Premark International] has been a spin-off addict ever since. As a director of Sears Roebuck (spinner of Allstate and Dean Witter Discover), Allstate, Temple-Inland (spun from Time Inc.), Cooper Industries (recidivist spinner) and Sprint (which just spun off its cellular business), Mr. Batts is to the corporate spin what Astaire was to the ballroom.

Parallels have been drawn with the Leveraged Buyout (LBO) movement of the 1980s. Robert Kitts of Morgan Stanley has singled out spin-offs as "the transaction of the year"; others are suggesting that this decade will be remembered for breakups, just as the 1980s was the decade of the LBO. It is not a wholly flattering comparison.

To some extent, LBOs were a financial engineering fad, dependent on the availability of junk bonds and their valuation. Initially, the junk-bond market was kick-started because Michael Milken was able to demonstrate that high-risk corporate paper was systematically undervalued. But by the time the LBO market exploded in the late 1980s, huge deals were being done because large quantities of junk bonds could be sold at prices that, with the benefit of hindsight, were too high. The junk bonds used to fuel many large and high-profile LBOs were actually riskier than thought at the time. When some of these LBOs ran into difficulties in the late 1980s, and many bondholders realized that they were sitting on genuine junk, the whole LBO movement, until then relentlessly increasing year by year, stalled and went into reverse.

We should therefore be cautious about dismissing the argument that breakups are, or at least could become, a fad. Nevertheless, our research does not support the view that breakups have come a fad. Most of the management groups initiating a breakup took a long time to decide on it. Indeed, many agreed to it only with the greatest reluctance. Emotional attachment to the old regime outweighed financial calculation. This may change, of course, as the financial success of breakups and their positive effect on the post-breakup morale of most managers become better appreciated.

SUMMARY AND CONCLUSION

All of the explanations for breakup that we have tested are unsatisfactory. Most of them are true, but do not go far enough. They tell us something about why breakups happen, but tell us little about the forces that lie behind the dramatic increases in value that we have observed.

Managers' desire for "more focus" (the standard answer) makes sense, but it is not a complete account of breakup. Sometimes, focus is invoked to provide a convenient rationale for a reversal of an earlier expansionist corporate strategy, for synergy that never arrived or turned negative. "Focus" is also a slippery concept: when are you focused enough? Can you have too much focus? How do we define it? How do you know when you have taken breakup far enough? We need a more specific concept than "focus" if we are to understand why and when breakup is justified. Focus is an appropriate goal, but it must be pursued with integrity and with a binding strategic logic. We show how in Chapter 5.

Managers' wish to raise the share price is also, as far as it goes, a sensible explanation of breakup. Since breakup usually does result in greater market value, it is an appropriate remedy for a weak share price. But why does breakup raise share prices? It is not good enough for corporate leaders simply to suggest that the market had it wrong before the breakup. The corporate financiers' explanation that the stock market likes "pure" investment vehicles helps to some degree. But why does the market like purity? Why are smaller pieces better? How many pieces should there be to be really pure? We come back to the same questions that were posed by the explanation of focus.

Fear of takeover, likewise, although sometimes the reason why breakup is undertaken, does not take us very far in understanding the root causes of breakup. Breakup can be an alternative to takeover, because it raises the share price. But why does it do this?

Other, more particular explanations, like using breakup to unwind a competitive conflict, cast some interesting light on corporate center strategies (usually, synergy that failed to arrive), but do not tell us the reason why breakup is so valuable in so many cases. And while some of the conditions for a fad are present, there is more to breakup than fashion.

Indeed many breakups are initiated for multiple reasons. Many of them are undertaken for two or three of the above reasons simultaneously. AT&T, always the biggest in everything it does, weighs in with four (see Exhibit 1).

Perhaps breakup has no common theme, no economic logic that explains why it is growing so fast. Perhaps it is just an aggregation of individual decisions which are more or less sensible. Perhaps there is simply no good general reason for breakup. We do not believe this is the case. We think there *is* more to breakup than has met the eye. In Chapter 3, we advance a new view, our general theory of breakup.

Exhibit 1

AT&T: PLENTY OF REASONS TO BREAK UP

In 1984, the US government forced AT&T to spin off its regional operating companies. In 1995, AT&T announced its second breakup, this time involving the spin-off of its manufacturing arm, now called Lucent, and its computer business, rechristened NCR. The revenues from these two businesses totaled approximately $33 billion. AT&T is thus the all time champion in the total size of its spin-offs.

The second breakup was a voluntary act, initiated primarily to escape an untenable internal conflict. The equipment business was losing orders on a large scale because its customers did not want to help a competitor—AT&T's long-distance service unit. It also provided the company with a way out of a disastrous foray into the computer business. AT&T's share price had been languishing before the announcement.

AT&T and the US government both have received a lot of flack over these transactions. Consumers and their representatives complained in the 1980s about the difficulty and inconvenience of buying telephone services from several companies simultaneously. Many observed that breaking up a telephone company that provided good service was probably the stupidest thing the government had ever done. Social observers were appalled at the huge layoffs—the Bell systems companies alone have shed some 200,000 employees since the 1984 divestiture. And financial observers note the several huge one-time charges associated with these layoffs and suggest that AT&T's performance has been less than sparkling. The company has indicated that another staffing reduction on the order of 40,000 will accompany this second breakup.

On the other hand, few customers now complain at the great variety of features and services they now enjoy with their telephones or the fall, in real terms, in virtually every tariff. And few investors can complain about a compound total return to investors of over 20 percent per annum since the first breakup. At that time, AT&T was worth some $47 billion. The total of the successor parts is now in excess of $300 billion. The 1984 breakup has been an undoubted success. The market believes this one will be as well and has reacted strongly to the announcement of the second breakup.

The current AT&T breakup was not only big, but it was laden with management motivation. This highly complex "trivestiture" was undertaken to (1) improve the focus on the core telecommunications services business in the face of major competitive battles ahead; (2) get the share price up after a long period in the doldrums; (3) remove a major competitive conflict; and (4) get rid of an embarrassingly poor performer.

Chapter 3

The Real Reason Why Breakup Creates Value

Breakups create value because they eliminate value destruction.

The forces of value destruction are ingrained in the
multibusiness corporation model.

Breakups create value because they eliminate value destruction. If businesses are worth less than the sum of their parts, there must be some loss of value in holding them together. If the simple act of breakup results in value creation, there must have been some value destruction for the breakup to eliminate. If the best strategy for a corporation is to break it into two or more pieces, there must be something wrong with the current structure or management approach.

Whereas many commentators see the reason for breakups in the new opportunities that are created, we argue that most breakups stem from underperformance caused by value destruction. This value destruction is not the fault of poor management teams or poor strategy (as conventionally defined). Value destruction is intrinsic and systemic to multibusiness companies (MBCs). The businesses get held back by their membership in the larger corporate entity. In the words of Gary Hamel and C.K. Prahalad in their best-seller, *Competing for the Future,* "the bottleneck is normally at the top of the bottle." The easiest, fastest, and most reliable way to remove the bottleneck is to break the bottle, allowing the separate pieces to perform without constraint.

In trade sales or takeovers, a change in ownership can create opportunities for a business that were not available under the previous regime. Trade sales and takeovers can therefore be justified by the logic of new value creation: new combinations allow beneficial change. But the justification of new opportunity cannot apply to breakups. When a business is broken into separate, stand-alone pieces with similar shareholders and the same managers, it is not possible to argue a logic of new value creation. Yet we can observe that the value after breakups is normally much greater than before. We can only explain this paradox as one of release from value destruction. There is no new positive force, just the removal of some negative ones; from the evidence, some pretty powerful ones at that.

In Chapter 2 we argued that most of the popular commentary on breakups is incomplete. We acknowledge that breakup is attractive because it seems to offer a sure-fire way to correct share price underperformance, that investors prefer pure plays, that some CEOs are running scared of predators, that breakups are more tax efficient than trades sales, that there is a danger that breakups could turn into financial engineering or corporate strategy fads, and that managers are often looking for increased focus. But these explanations are inadequate because they fail to expose the fundamental economic drivers behind the breakup phenomenon. The real reason, the basic economic driver, is that most MBCs are destroying value, by their very nature. Breakup is usually the easiest, least painful, and least revolutionary way to put an end to this value destruction.

THE LOGIC FOR MULTIBUSINESS COMPANIES

To understand why value destruction is the driving force behind the breakup phenomenon, we need to stand back and consider why MBCs exist in the first place.

Like any economic entity that grows and prospers in a free-market system, MBCs exist for good reasons. MBCs are created because successful businesses generate cash; successful managers want to replicate that success by spending the cash to expand. Seeing their horizons limited in their company's original business, they want to grow, to spread risk, to build adjacent businesses. If they do not fail in their initial forays, over time they build the original small, focused business into a large diversified corporation, embracing multiple businesses, often in more than one industry, and on several continents.

Let's take a typical MBC as shown in Figure 17. It has three divisions—a manufacturing division, a retailing division, and a hotel division—and a total of ten operating businesses. Each of these businesses is large enough to be an independent company in its own right. There is a management hierarchy consisting of division level heads, and a corporate HQ complete with its own staff and group CEO. Those people at HQ and at division levels are what we term the "corporate center."

FIGURE 17
A Typical Multibusiness Company (MBC)

The Corporate Center

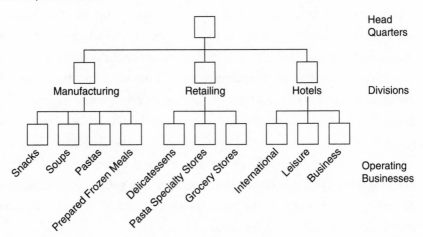

The issue we are trying to understand is: why does it make sense to have these ten businesses reporting to a corporate center? When is it best to have an MBC? Alternately, when would it be better to perform a breakup and abolish the corporate center? Then again, if the decision is to break up, should the breakup create three new companies—the previous divisions—or ten independent businesses, each now with its own shareholders and bankers? Or some other structure?

If the grouping of ten operating businesses under one center is to be justified on economic grounds, it must be on the basis that the businesses in aggregate will do better as a group than they would as three or ten independent firms. To justify one company, the corporate center—both the head office and the three divisional head offices, taken together—must add value to the individual operating companies.

Now, both in theory and in practice, it is not hard for a center to add value. By combining into one group, the company is likely to be able to reduce the cost of borrowing. It can also save certain administrative costs in specialist financial areas like the production of annual financial statements and communicating with the capital markets. If the offsetting costs of the corporate center can be kept to a level below that of the savings, the net result will be positive. On the surface, therefore, groups of businesses make sense.

Beyond financial matters, the center can potentially add value to the operating companies in many other ways. It can advise and guide, bringing in experienced and capable managers whom it would be beyond the ability of any individual operating company to attract or pay. It can provide human-resource support to raise the quality of management and train staff. It can lower the cost of some goods and services by centralizing their purchase. Using internal resources, it can back exciting new developments more quickly and more heavily than if the operating companies had to do the rounds of external financiers. It can appoint new CEOs who are better than their predecessors and better than the operating companies themselves would have been capable of picking. Clearly there are many ways that a wise center can add value to its businesses and justify itself economically. Almost any center, even if not very well run, is bound to add *some* value.

So, to develop a logic for breakups, for example, by breaking off the manufacturing division of our MBC, we must argue the presence of value destruction. If some value is added by the manufacturing division's membership in the group—as is almost certainly the case—we must argue that a still greater amount of value is being destroyed. Otherwise the breakups could not make economic sense. We must argue that the manufacturing businesses are being held back in some way by their membership of the wider group. We must argue that, even though the manufacturing businesses will have to incur some additional administrative and financing costs, they will still perform better. Why? Because they will be released from some constraints inherent in belonging to the group; they will no longer be under some damaging influence; nor will they be able to build services and supports that are more effectively tailored to their needs. If this is not true, we cannot justify the breakup. To argue the logic of the breakup, we need to argue for the existence of value destruction.

And, since we posit that the value created by a group is often substantial; and that the net benefits of breakups are, in most cases, very substantial; we have to argue that the amounts of value destroyed by many MBCs are more substantial still.

It so happens that this is the case.

VALUE DESTRUCTION

Ashridge Strategic Management Centre has been researching the value added by MBCs since 1987. The focus has been on learning how centers add value and how the value they add can be increased. The research involved scouring the world for examples of best practice, of centers that add the most value in their industries or in their type of MBC. But perhaps the Centre has been engaged in the wrong task. For the results are clear: all centers add some value—and typically quite large amounts of value—to the operating companies they own. Moreover, there are also benefits that arise from bringing businesses together that involve little influence or action by the center. Yet despite this positive starting point many centers destroy substantially more value than they add. While a few MBCs create substantial net value (that is, they create more than they destroy), many do not; and many more, in fact the large majority, are net value destroyers in at least part of their portfolio. This disturbing conclusion, based on studying a large number of MBCs in many different countries and cultures, casts serious doubt on whether MBCs can and should continue to play their dominant role in business and society.

Value destruction is not confined to conglomerates, currently deeply out of favor with investors and caricatured in the media as artificial financial engineering constructs. Oddly, some of the companies traditionally regarded as highly diverse actually possess some powerful group value added: their corporate centers are net value creators. But even companies with portfolios in a single industry, or in a series of apparently related areas, are frequently net value destroyers. Value destruction is not just the result of a lack of focus. Rather, it stems from the relationship between the center and the operating companies it owns.

THE CENTER AS AN INTERMEDIARY

Centers of MBCs are curious things. As Figure 18 shows, in contrast to the operating businesses, the corporate center of an MBC does not have external customers and so cannot generate wealth. The center has costs, but not revenues. Primary wealth creation occurs only at the level of the operating business. The operating businesses, if they are viable, could obtain funding without going to their center. They could go to venture capitalists, bankers, and/or, if big enough, directly to the stock market. It follows that the center is an optional intermediary. If the center did not exist, it would not be necessary to invent it. It exists; it owns the businesses; but it need not do so.

The corporate center is a middleman, an intermediary between the providers of finance and the operating businesses. It does not have an automatic right to exist. It can only be justified economically if it adds more value than it subtracts. In many cases, the net is negative for at least a major part of the portfolio. In other words, value destruction often exceeds value creation. Why? What causes so much value destruction?

FIGURE 18

The Center of MBCs as an Intermediary

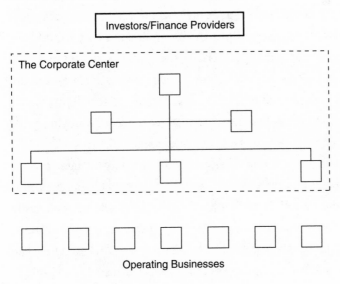

VALUE DESTROYER 1: EXECUTIVE INFLUENCE

All corporate centers exercise a powerful influence on the businesses they own. The center agrees to targets, discusses strategy, approves or disapproves requests for capital, monitors performance, gives advice, and appoints the head of each business. The latter would behave differently and make different decisions if he or she were independent. Executive influence can be highly beneficial, but tends to be negative, often very negative. How come?

Lack of Fit Between Owner and Owned

One very obvious cause of value destruction is lack of fit between the center and the businesses it owns. Put crudely, the center does not understand the businesses it owns, and so will make worse decisions about them than would be made by the executives running the companies by themselves. Lack of fit is surprisingly prevalent.

Let's examine an extreme example to make the point. Take the oil industry. Oil firms around the world have tried diversification into almost every single business you could name. Amazingly, without a single notable success. You might have thought that just by rolling the dice they would have had some successes. But, almost universally, they fail. Given the number of tries, the odds against this happening just through bad luck are astronomical. It couldn't have happened by chance. So, given the money thrown at diversification, the oil companies must have been actively destroying value with enormous consistency to achieve this outcome.

We are not talking about unprofessional, stupid, or fly-by-night companies. When corporations with highly intelligent, dedicated professionals, such as Exxon, Shell, and British Petroleum (BP) diversified into minerals in the 1980s, it seemed a sensible choice. The move was generally applauded at the time by the financial community. The oil companies believed they had the appropriate skills to make a success of minerals because, like oil, minerals involved exploration, extraction, negotiations with difficult governments, technically complex projects, and large amounts of capital. In the currently fashionable jargon, minerals and oil seemed to share core competencies: they appeared to be related businesses.

Yet, after a decade of disillusionment, oil companies have beaten a retreat from minerals. BP sold its minerals business to the RTZ Corporation in 1989, and recently Shell sold its operations to South Africa's Gencor. Why? Because they made a botch of it. The minerals businesses of Atlantic Richfield, BP, Exxon, Shell, and Standard Oil had an average pretax return on sales of minus 17 percent during the mid-1980s. Over the same period, independent minerals companies were making a plus 10 percent return. That is, the oil majors were achieving a staggering net 27 percent lower return than their focused rivals—about as large a gap as you can find in margins between competitors anywhere. Why were the oil companies so good at destroying value?

One manager in BP's minerals operation explained to us: "The problem was that the BP managing directors could not really come to grips with the minerals business or feel they understood it. There was always that vestige of suspicion that led to a temptation to say no to proposals from the business, or, alternatively, if they said yes, to say yes for the wrong reasons."

With hindsight, we can see that the success factors in minerals were different from those in oil. Exploration in minerals is not as critical. More important is access to low-cost deposits because only these make a profit in the down-cycles. In minerals, forming joint ventures with companies that already have low-cost mines can be more profitable than searching for new deposits. Pressure from oil company executives to spend more on exploration proved counterproductive.

Despite the superficial logic of common core competencies and similar products, oil and minerals did not mix. This is not atypical. Whether the center and all its businesses fit well is a question that few people at the center tend to address. But if the fit is not good, the decisions that are made will be poorer than if the center did not exist. All successful business people carry around in their heads insights, rules of thumb, and mental maps that have been built up through a lifetime's experience of trial and error. The insights, rules of thumb, and mental maps generally work well, enabling quick and appropriate decisions. But as the oil companies' forays into minerals proved, they are not universal. They are conditioned by particular experiences. Applied in other fields, they can prove wrong. Even slight differences can be expensive.

The 10 Percent Versus 100 Percent Paradox

Lack of fit is only one reason why the center tends to destroy value through its own influence. There is a basic and unavoidable problem with the center's influence. To improve performance, executive influence must result in different and better decisions than the team dedicated to running the business would have reached. But why should the group CEO, in 10 percent of his or her time, be able to see better ways forward than energetic managers who devote 100 percent of their time to the business and are familiar with all its nuances? Almost always, those at the center must be less well informed and not as close to the needs of the business's customers than those in the front line. However highly qualified, ocean-going captains need local pilots to help them navigate the peculiarities of the local coastline. It is only in rare circumstances that the ocean-going captains can give advice to the local pilots.

The Truth Possession and Perversion Paradox

To make better decisions, those at the center must be at least as well informed as those in the operating companies. Yet most of their information and understanding of a business will be derived from the managers in the business itself. Unless the center uses expensive consultants and market researchers to build up an independent and superior proprietary database, it will be hard to second guess the operating managers. If the data are obtained from the business itself, it is a matter of definition that those at the center will be less well informed: the center's information will be incomplete.

This is mainly because there are insidious incentives for managers to pass on misleading data. This perversion of truth takes many different forms and happens for many different reasons. There may be a crisis in the business that the operating managers want to conceal or downplay. There may be good news that is obscured in the interests of not raising expectations. Or the good news may be exaggerated in the hope of gathering immediate credit. If businesses think they are competing against each other internally for finite investment funds, they may slant information and proposals to gain approval or, even worse, adjust sensible plans to take into account the center's known predilections. Most notorious of all cases of incomplete and misleading information is the annual budget negotiation. The business managers are negotiating for their bonus—they may have $50,000 at stake. If they can persuade the center that the outlook is bad, that reengineering will only have a minor impact on costs, and that there is a shortage of product developments in the pipeline, they may be able to reduce their budget target by enough to double their bonus at year's end. It would test the morality of a saint to declare all information at budget time.

The Alienation Syndrome

Human beings work harder and smarter if they believe they are in control of their own destinies. Improvisation, going the extra mile for customers, adapting quickly to changed circumstances, and making business decisions based on the needs of customers, are all more natural and effective when executives are free to do it their way. This is often harder to arrange when a business is owned by a corporate center. The parent corporation casts a long shadow; and however enlightened and decentralized it is, however much empowerment, involvement, and participation it promotes, the danger of alienation is ever present.

The Insulation Syndrome

Businesses that are part of a well-heeled MBC may not feel the same urgency to perform as independent companies. Within the security of the corporation, and keen to assert an equivalent right to resources as that enjoyed by any other part of the corporation, managers harbor unnecessary costs; avoid risky price increases; gold-plate investments; dampen down expectations, budgets, and targets; tolerate loss-making products, customers, territories, and distribution channels; use more working capital than is necessary; and fail to search out the best opportunities for profitable growth. Almost everyone who works in an MBC knows that this happens; almost no one bothers to calculate the profit impact. Usually the impact is a substantial proportion of current profits; but not infrequently it is a multiple of current profits.

How do we know this? Partly from our consulting experience, where we have been able to document the profit impact of specific actions taken or not taken, and where we have helped corporations remove inappropriate cross-subsidies and raise performance targets. But we are working against the grain. The structure of the MBC is inherently unfriendly toward the profit maximizer. The gains are always hard work and often transitory.

In one large US company, we calculated the value creation potential of two alternative strategies for a particular business unit. Even the worst-case outcome of these strategies was better than the best-case outcome of the steady-as-we-go strategy it was pursuing. When we confronted the business chief executive, he said that he had always suspected that these alternatives were better, but he had not pushed for them because of the way the center discouraged risk taking. "If I put forward your best option, my target for the next three years would be set at or close to the best-case outcome. Even on your calculations, I am unlikely to achieve that. Hence, I would be setting myself up for failure. The way we set targets in this company forces us to stick to the known, the plannable, the deliverable. It's wrong, but it's reality."

The more powerful and persuasive evidence of the insulation syndrome comes when the structure of the MBC is abolished, either through a Leveraged or Management Buyout (LBO/MBO), or through a breakup. The damage caused by the influence of the center can be seen clearly in the MBO experience, where the main change is the shift in management control and the elimination of the center rather than financial structure. For good and ill, it forces the business to stand on its own feet and make its own decisions. Behavior nearly always changes greatly.

A case in point is Premier Brands, created by the buyout by British managers in 1986 of Cadbury-Schweppes food interests. Paul Judge, a career manager with Cadbury, led the buyout. When it was part of Cadbury, he told us, there had been a feeling that, despite moderate results, the division was protected. Once Premier became independent, the whole work force was aware that performance had to improve. Headcount was reduced by a quarter, working capital was halved, there was a new sense of urgency, profits rose from £6.6 million in 1985 to £31 million in 1988, and the business was sold in 1989 for more than three times the total funding cost, creating large fortunes for the managers.

Executive influence is a powerful force in multibusiness companies. It can be positive, when the managers at the top understand the problems of managers lower down and know how to help them. Very often, however, executive influence is not positive. The lack of understanding, the 10 percent versus 100 percent paradox, the truth-perversion paradox, the alienation syndrome, and the insulation syndrome overwhelm the good intentions and dedicated hard work of the managers at the center. In these cases the net is negative, and can be very negative.

VALUE DESTROYER 2: LINKAGE INITIATIVES

Value in MBCs is typically also destroyed through linkage initiatives: the process of encouraging interaction between the businesses in the portfolio. Linkage initiatives start out with high hopes of finding and exploiting synergy. But they often end in disgruntlement, recriminations, and bad feeling. Mark Sirower, a management theorist at New York University, entitled his study of the subject *The Synergy Trap*. Acquisition deals driven by the logic of synergy have two features, he argues: the acquiring company pays too much for the target; and the synergies fail to materialize.

Work by the Ashridge Strategic Management Centre uses the word "mirage" to communicate to management the nature of the pitfall. The corporate center often sees synergies that are not there. They shimmer seductively, an apparent oasis almost in reach. Corporate center managers whip up excitement on a premise of piles of gold, competitive advantage, and the warm glow of teamwork and the corporate good. Once shown the mirage, business managers can become equally animated. Committees, project teams, transfer pricing mechanisms, matrices, centralization, and coordination are prescribed. But the gold, the competitive advantage, and the warm glow recede faster than the managers can move to grasp them. Gradually, individual businesses start to do less well because energy has been diverted from the task of keeping them ahead of their markets. Finally, all involved feel deceived and disappointed.

We are not saying that all linkage initiatives fail. There are many situations of successful coordination. For example, joint purchasing or coordinated manufacturing can lower operating costs; coordinated strategies toward customers can help protect margins; and shared research and development can raise the quality of products or services. The overall result, however, is strikingly similar. Just as we identified more anergy than synergy, more value destruction than value creation, so we find more mirage than oasis. The question again is: Why?

Corporate Center Bias

The first reason why center managers see mirages is that they have a perception bias. Synergy, like any new activity, is not easily pinned down by cost/benefit analysis. The benefits are hard to estimate in advance, and the costs, particularly opportunity costs (i.e., the value that is lost from diverting management time from some other activity), difficult to assess. If you plan to create synergy from a single brand name across a number of businesses in different countries, how do you estimate costs and benefits? You can probably judge the cost of converting other brands to a single name. But you can't estimate the increase in sales this will cause. And you can't estimate what sales will be lost as a result of distracting management time from alternative initiatives.

This uncertainty about costs and benefits adds luster to mirages, especially if managers are actively looking for synergies; and most corporate center managers are. Corporate center managers are always looking for ways of bringing their group of businesses more closely together, tying family knots, and justifying the existence of the group. They have been taught by academics and consultants that the answer lies in synergy. The group makes sense if two plus two equals more than four. So, center managers are desperate to find synergy. As they peer at the businesses through the inadequate lenses of their cost/benefit binoculars, they imagine synergy that doesn't exist: they see mirages.

Why don't business managers point this out? Why don't they correct the cost/benefit analysis and point out that neither the rainbow nor the crock of gold exists? The answer is that the business-unit manager is also looking for a justification for the corporate whole. He or she also wants to bond with the rest of the family and find common cause. Hence the emotional desire to believe the corporate center manager. "We thought he could see something we couldn't," explained one bemused business manager. "We were seduced into believing in the 'one enterprise' concept," commented another. "We wanted to find synergy too," pointed out another. As a result business managers often do not challenge the validity of the initiative.

When they do, they are mostly ignored. Worse, they are criticized for negative behavior. "Parochial thinking," is the response. Not-invented-here accusations are quickly leveled at the gainsayer. "Not a team player." "Only interested in the success of his own unit." "Doesn't seem to be able to take a group view." "No vision." "Can't seem to wear a group hat." For the true believer, there are many ways to convince him- or herself that the mirage is real and that those who cannot see it are short-sighted, blinkered, or self-interested cynics.

Enlightened Self-interest Paradox

Self-interested behavior is in fact the whole basis of our successful market economy. By failing to value self-interest and by viewing it as short-sighted or cynical, center managers compound the problem. They double the chances of seeing mirages.

The business of business is acting for self-interested reasons. The beauty of the market system is that it is hard to do business without fulfilling someone else's interest at the same time. There are two parties to every transaction. Both must want to do business. Both must see some self-interested benefit from the transaction.

The unique skill of business people is their ability to find sets of transactions that they can carry out with other business people, or with consumers, that advance the success of their business. Managers are continually searching for new transactions, for new people to do business with, for new ways of doing business. They buy, sell, license, borrow, share, swap, lend, joint-venture, partner, benchmark, and form alliances with other managers all the time. They are experts at the business of linking with other businesses, suppliers, and customers to create value out of the transactions that result. Their self-interested behavior pushes them into relationships of all kinds. Like hyperactive children, they cannot control their urge to transact.

Why then should there be money on the table? Why should the center suppose that the managers in the businesses are not already linking with each other to the optimum degree? As enlightened managers (and if not enlightened they need to be changed) pursuing their desire to transact, profit, and extend their influence, we should expect any piles of gold to be gained from coordinating within the family to be spotted and quickly captured. Only if you assume that business-unit managers are willfully choosing not to do business with each other do you need linkage initiatives sponsored by the center.

Interestingly there *are* good reasons why business managers choose not to transact with sister companies. Often the reasons are created by the existence of the corporate center, by past attempts of the center to force inappropriate coordination, and by fear of the center's insensitive, hard-charging behavior. The old saying, "never do business with the family," exists for good reason. Business transactions that go wrong cause bad feeling. Between businesses transacting at arm's length, this bad feeling can be dissipated. If the conflict gets too fierce the relationship can be terminated and another set up in its place.

Between business family members, the downside risks of bad feeling are much greater. The individual on the other side of the transaction may have been a colleague for twenty years or more. He or she may be a future boss or subordinate. He or she may report your behavior to influential people and interfere with your career progress. On top of that, the corporate center may descend like Solomon and stop the fighting with an arbitrary solution that leaves you worse off. Doing business with the family has dangers. If you ask a classroom of managers how many prefer doing business with outside organizations rather than with the family, 100 percent will raise their hands and vote in favor. The corporate center inhibits linkages just by its existence. Think of it like this: To create value from linkage, the corporate center must overcome its natural disadvantage, find areas where enlightened self-interest is not working, confirm that the pot of gold is not a mirage, and then work to bring the parties together in a successful transaction. It's a tall order. Not surprisingly there are more failures than successes.

VALUE DESTROYER 3: CENTRAL STAFFS

The third source of value destruction is the existence of staff departments at the corporate center. These staff departments are an essential part of most corporate centers. They normally include the finance functions like tax, treasury, and financial control. They can also include other functions such as public relations, legal, personnel, research, engineering, and so on.

Good corporate center staffs and service departments can create value. They can help corporate center managers, advise business managers, and carry out common services more efficiently or more skillfully. However, they often don't.

These service departments and functions are a well-documented source of problems. In most companies they are under attack and for good reason. The policies they impose on the portfolio are frequently inappropriate, the services they provide are unresponsive, and their influence on the corporate psyche is disempowering.

Inappropriate Policies

Corporate departments create policies. The finance department requires that financial figures are submitted by the fourth working day after the end of the month. The human resources function develops policies for salary structures, bonus systems, car entitlement, training, and so on. The public relations people require review of all press statements before release. The senior vice president for marketing sets policies for the use of the corporate brand and gives advice on advertising agencies. The lawyers check every contract. Every staff department creates policies. Even strategic planners define plan format and submission frequency and who should attend strategic planning events.

All these policies are developed with the best of intentions. Staff managers genuinely believe that policy will raise standards, lower costs, improve control, or ease transfer of management between businesses. For a variety of reasons, they are frequently and almost inevitably wrong.

They are wrong because central staff managers have a limited perspective: they cannot be sufficiently knowledgeable about all the businesses to know the impact of each policy on each business. Moreover, their thinking is biased by the views of the most powerful businesses. As any staff manager knows, the best way to get a corporate policy agreed to is to win the backing of the most important divisional leaders. Again, they are misled because they start with the assumption of one policy for all. Policy development is hard enough without having to do it separately for individual businesses. In any case, staff managers are believers in professionalism and best practice, so they want all businesses to live up to the central standard. Staff managers rarely have front-line understanding of the delicate trade-offs, the peculiar economics, or the special standards that distinguish different market places. They are reinforced in their beliefs by powerful concepts of unity: one company, one enterprise, one culture, one oneness.

One company spent millions of dollars developing a new corporate logo and defining the common features in the company's culture. Convinced of the special nature of the company's culture, senior executives wanted to capture its essence, reinforce the strengths, and improve the weaknesses. It proved impossible. Attempts to describe the culture were never satisfactory. Like a portrait painter who isn't quite able to catch the sitter's likeness, the consultants failed to put the intangible on paper to the satisfaction of the top management team.

Three years later the company broke in two, and the reason for the consultants' failure became transparently clear. One manager explained: "We were schizoid. It was not until we separated that we realized how much effort was going into trying to create a common culture. We were forever compromising and trying to be alike. Now we are two companies, the cultures have literally leapt apart and are accelerating away from each other. It would be impossible to put it back together without a bloodbath."

Unresponsive Services

Central service departments are disappearing under pressure from outsourcing, divisionalizing, and decentralizing. Where they exist, central services are often major value destroyers.

A central services department only makes sense if it can outperform the alternatives—if it can do a better job than an outsourced service provider, and also do a better job than managers located within the business unit.

The traditional arguments have concerned economies of scale (by centralizing it is possible to make better use of specialist resources) or the ability to attract better quality people (if each business unit recruited its own treasurer, the average quality would decline). Clearly there are situations where these arguments make sense. But, with the rise of external service providers in fields ranging from strategic planning to invoicing, and from pensions to tax management, the situations are becoming rarer. To justify itself the central service must perform better than the external professional and better than the local manager, tailoring itself to the needs of any specific business. This is a tough challenge.

The criticism of central services, however, is not mainly that they are noncompetitive. The emotion that surrounds central services and the energy that is going into their dismemberment directly reflect the realization that many of them are much worse than noncompetitive: they are actively destructive. Why?

The reason for their bad performance is their privileged status. As central services, they are protected from the winds of competition, the tantrums of customers, and the demands of unreasonable bosses. Like the soft carpeted hallways of most corporate offices, central services become cosseted, padded with unnecessary costs, and distant from their customers.

The problem is hard to eliminate. The central service usually makes sense only if all or most of the businesses use it. So power is immediately removed from the customer (the operating business), who has little leverage over poor service. The central service also usually reports to a corporate center manager who has little knowledge of the operations of the service and little interest in becoming an expert. The VP for finance has bigger fish to fry than becoming an expert in invoicing or systems development. The CEO has little interest in being an expert in public relations or strategic-planning processes. The SVP of human resources has no enthusiasm for being an expert in pension management. Without knowledgeable bosses to breathe down their necks, and with disempowered customers who prefer to use their political chips on bigger issues, central services not only lose the competitive edge but lose sight of their objectives. They become committed to a self-serving agenda that begins to erode the competitiveness of the businesses they are serving.

Central IT departments frequently reduce the competitiveness of the business units they are supposed to serve. They pursue central agenda items, such as system compatibility, central purchasing, and advanced systems technology, at the expense of the commercial needs of the businesses. They advise the units to develop systems that support the central agenda but are inappropriate in competitive terms.

Stories in other departments abound. One multibusiness retailer had a central security department, peopled by experts on customer pilfering, surveillance systems, and security guarding. A new acquisition was instructed to end its current security arrangements in favor of the central service. Confident of reducing "wastage" by 1 percent or more, the latter recommended new labor-saving surveillance equipment and additional in-store guarding. But "wastage" increased by more than 1 percent, costing the company $2½ million on top of $½ million spent on surveillance equipment and $100,000 on extra guarding costs. Only after extensive management debate and a damaging erosion of trust between the group CEO and the business president, was it discovered that the main cause of "wastage" in this business was not customers but staff. In this context, the "expertise" of the central security department had been a disadvantage rather than a benefit.

Disempowering Influence

Nothing is more frustrating to the business manager than the bureaucracy, lack of responsiveness, ignorance, and continual demands for information that usually characterize central staffs. As consultants we have witnessed this frustration first hand many times. As researchers we have filing cabinets bulging with the quotes of outraged managers:

> How could they do this to me? They knew the mailing had to go out in June. They told me there was no problem with it. And their excuse—an urgent corporate mailing coincided with an unexpected staff illness and a decision by the marketing SVP to review priorities. But the worst is that they didn't tell me until it was too late to arrange something else.

Had it been an external supplier, the manager could have eased his frustration by complaining at the highest level, withholding payment, or moving to another supplier. With an internal service department the feeling of disempowerment can be overwhelming.

We are not trying to suggest that all central staffs are deliberately incompetent. Some nearly always get good ratings. The tax function and the treasury function are usually well appreciated by business-level managers. But, it is common for most staff departments to be under attack. This is because it is hard for them to avoid disempowering, being unresponsive, and developing inappropriate policies.

VALUE DESTROYER 4: PORTFOLIO DEVELOPMENT

The last source of value destruction is a set of activities normally described as portfolio development. These involve acquisitions, divestments, corporate venturing initiatives, and efforts to define or dramatically reshape particular businesses. We will focus here particularly on acquisitions.

Beating the Odds

Countless academic research projects have been carried out on the subject of acquisitions. The conclusions are consistent and irrefutable. Most acquisitions destroy value for the acquiring company. Most of the value released from the change in ownership (if there is value to be released) goes to the seller, not the buyer.

The pace of acquisition activity speaks volumes for the eternal optimism that fuels the process. Yet at some level, most managers understand the odds. Even the language recognizes the reality. As the term "acquisition premium" implies, the discussion does not focus on whether there will be a premium, but on how big it will be: 10 percent is low. 30 percent is common. 100 percent is not unheard of. What does this mean? It means that the buyer is paying a premium over and above the value of the business in its current state. It is paying the premium to persuade the seller to sell, and to sell to the bidder rather than to some other company looking to expand in the same area.

The logic is sound. If there is no premium, there is no reason for the seller to sell. On the other hand, there is little reason for the buyer to buy unless there is an opportunity to improve the target's "current state." To conclude the transaction, the buyer needs to give away some of the improvement he or she is hoping to create, to tempt the seller and to beat off other buyers. Sometimes the buyer has to give away most of the expected improvement. This happens when two or more buyers can see the same potential for improvement. Inevitably there are occasions when the final price includes not only a premium on the current state but a premium on the expected improved state. Buyers sometimes continue the bidding just "to prevent a rival from getting the deal."

The net result of this "sound logic" is that the deal itself destroys value: a premium has been paid. Afterwards, the new owner attempts to improve operations sufficiently to justify the price paid—by exerting executive influence, launching linkage initiatives, and applying the expertise of central staffs. The result? Well, some value is always added. But as we have explained, value is often destroyed. The net may be positive, but it is rarely greater than the premium. The net is often negative, compounding the error. The acquisition not only destroys value through the premium paid, but also multiplies the error by destroying more value through poor executive influence or linkage initiatives.

Sony's venture into Hollywood is an example of these forces at work, not only in the glare of public attention, but also in financial terms that make

Arnold Schwarzenegger look like a bargain. The late Senator Everett Dirksen was credited with the quote: "A billion here and a billion there and very soon you are talking serious money." This is serious money indeed. Rough calculations show that Sony paid a billion or two more than it should have for the ailing Columbia Studios and has thrown a few billion more after that as a result of choosing the wrong people, applying the wrong controls, and pushing wrong-headed ideas about the software/hardware synergies. Only a breakup or trade sale can resolve a problem that has so far cost it between $4 billion and $8 billion. Yet Sony persists in its Oscar-winning demonstration of how acquisitions destroy value.

Corporate Ambition

CEOs and chairmen like size. They are instinctive expansionists who dream of making their companies the biggest, the most successful companies in the land. Who should deny them their dreams? Our economy needs people like this. Ambition is not to be sneered at.

But corporate ambition brings problems. In the case of acquisition, the problems lie in the difficulty of valuing a company. What is a company worth? It is worth a multiple of what it can earn. What can it earn? That in turn depends on assumptions made about the future economy, the actions of competitors, the likelihood of it developing major new products, and so on. The real answer is that we don't know what it can earn within an accuracy of more than plus or minus about 50 percent of what it is currently earning: the future is uncertain.

Let's put this into numbers. If the company is earning $10 million today, and we expect that to remain consistent forever, we might be confident in valuing it at five times earnings (i.e., $50 million). But if we can't be sure whether the company will earn $5 million or $15 million, and we can't be sure how fast these earnings will grow in the future, we are unsure whether it is worth $25 million or $75 million. If we are optimistic, particularly if we believe we can influence events, we might be comfortable valuing it at $75 million or even $100 million. In our acquisition plan, our "walk-away" price might be set at $70 million. But if the real value, the value that can only be put on the business with hindsight, is only $30 million, we may end up tossing $40 million away.

Corporate ambition says: "We want the business. We can expect the business to do well under our leadership. The future is positive." As a result, the walk-away price may be set at $70 million. If more than one bidder is involved, particularly if they are rivals in the industrial pecking order, both will be prepared to sacrifice walk-away prices. The result is horrifying but predictable: whoever wins will have paid too much.

In current markets, this often happens. Companies seeking to sell retain a sales adviser: a bank or an accountant. The bank prepares an eloquent "sales memorandum" and seeks prospective buyers. With luck, twenty expressions of interest will come in and this will be narrowed down to five or six serious, qualified bidders. Then the auction starts.

If buyers normally overpay, isn't it best to be a seller? Unfortunately, here again corporate ambition can stand in the way. Managers do not think of themselves as sellers. Selling is a sign of failure. Selling is rarely seen as a positive step forward. Selling has little to recommend it, except that it normally creates value!

Corporate ambition can therefore get in the way of sound portfolio development. Unless portfolio decisions are well targeted, value is often destroyed. Corporate center managers need to understand which businesses are worth more to their company than to rival bidders. It is only for these businesses that they can afford to outbid rivals.

Center managers also need to understand which businesses are likely to be worth more to rival bidders. These are good businesses to sell.

SUMMARY: VALUE DESTRUCTION, MBCS, AND BREAKUPS

We started by arguing that it is easy for corporate centers to add value. They can reduce the cost of borrowing. They can save administrative costs such as the production of annual financial statements and communicating with analysts. They can generate tax benefits. They can provide expertise in treasury, pensions, or human resources legislation. We recognize that these sources of value are often quite sufficient to pay for modest central costs. The problem with the MBC is not the cost of the center. It is not the dedication, willingness, and determination of the center managers. It is the framework in which they are operating.

We estimate that the act of creating a multibusiness corporation nearly always destroys at least 10 per cent of the value of the stand-alone component parts. And in many cases, it destroys many times that figure—50 percent or more. We have arrived at our 10 percent judgment based on the following:

• The cost of headquarters: data from a 1993 study by the Ashridge Strategic Management Centre ("Effective Headquarters Staff," by David Young and Michael Goold) suggest that corporate centers typically cost on the order of 1% of sales; for a company earning 10 percent on sales, this amounts to 10 percent of profits, and hence 10 percent of the combined entity's value.

• Diversity discount: JP Morgan's study of American conglomerates shows that the "conglomerate discount" imputed by the stock market over the past ten years has ranged between 10 and 20 percent. Companies pay a big penalty by being diverse. This is because: (1) the market appears to like purity; it is not clear why this is the case or what the lack-of-purity discount is; but evidence from investment trusts and closed-end funds suggests that it is significant—perhaps a few percent; (2) companies that would be acquired if independent forgo an acquisition premium when "locked up" inside a portfolio of a company known to be a buyer, not a seller; and (3) the market senses our third argument—unavoidable bureaucracy.

• Unavoidable bureaucracy: even in good multibusiness companies, there is some unavoidable bureaucracy. An extra layer of management cannot avoid slowing down some decision processes, confusing some motivations and accountabilities, and distracting some management time from products and customers. It is hard to estimate the size of this unavoidable value destruction, but few managers believe it is zero.

It is worth emphasizing what we are saying here. We believe that every multibusiness company, even the good ones (the FBCs), are fighting an uphill battle. If you ignore the positive influence of the corporate center, the combined entity would be worth at least 10 percent less. The cost of the center, the lack of purity discount, the loss of acquisition premiums, and the unavoidable bureaucracy are costs inherent in the multibusiness model.

Managers at the center must believe that they can add at least 10 percent to have any claim for existence. To be reasonably confident that their influence will be net positive, they need to make a case for 20 percent added value.

In most of the breakup cases we have examined, the value destruction is much greater than 10 percent. This is because the headquarters costs are high, the loss of acquisition premiums is large, bureaucracy is a major problem, and, in addition, the center is giving inappropriate guidance to the businesses and/or there is friction between the businesses. These last two categories of value destruction, inappropriate guidance and friction, can account for 50 percent or more value destruction. AT&T bought NCR for $7 billion and subsequently spun it off for less than half this value. An academic study of the NCR situation concludes that all of the value destruction was due to the bad influences of AT&T. AT&T paid too much for NCR in the first place and then gave NCR bad guidance over the years of its ownership. Another dramatic example is that of Sears, where its total market capitalization rose from $8 billion to $42 billion as a result of its series of breakups. All companies need to overcome the inherent costs and penalties of the multibusiness model. The major breakups are the result of the systematic value destruction caused by inappropriate guidance or friction between businesses.

It is of course possible to create a lot of value in the center. But those companies which are net value creators start with a 10 percent penalty and must avoid any substantial value destruction of the sort set out above or the net will be negative. That is why most MBCs destroy net value and should be broken up.

Our conclusion here is central. The MBC model destroys value. It does so in a pervasive way that is hard to stop and hard to measure. It is in the fabric of the organization model. Offsetting this value destruction is value creation. However, unless corporate center managers have a clear understanding of the value they are trying to create, and focus on creating it, the net is often negative. The MBC model is an expensive way to run a company. It should only be used if there is a strong reason for it: if center managers have a clear understanding of why it will create more value than it destroys.

Are we saying that all MBCs must disappear? No. Are we saying that all corporate centers are bad? No. Are we saying that the future lies only in single businesses? No. We are saying that many MBCs need to be broken up. And we are saying that the MBC model should be used sparingly. Breakup is at epidemic levels because the MBC model is being misused. There is a trillion dollar opportunity because the MBC model is being imposed on businesses and clusters of businesses that would do much better without it.

The MBC will continue to be needed for some situations. The focused business company (FBC) is where the future of MBCs lies. In the FBC there are still multiple businesses and a center. The multibusiness model still destroys value but, in an FBC, the relationship between the center and the businesses creates enough value to more than offset the model's disadvantage.

We can illustrate these points by returning to the example of the Food and Hotel Corporation shown earlier in Figure 17. Should this conglomerate, currently with three divisions and ten operating companies, end up as three breakups, ten, or a number in between? What is the correct answer?

We describe the analyses that should be done to reach the correct answer in Chapter 4, but we can address the question in its broad outline here. Are we saying that the only solution is to create ten separate businesses, however small and insignificant they are? No. What we are crusading against is value destruction, not size.

The Food and Hotel Corporation should break up in such a way that it eliminates as much value destruction as possible without throwing the baby out with the bath water; without losing any significant value creation that may come from executive influence, linkage initiatives, and central staffs. Our instinct would be to create one FBC from the food manufacturing division. We would expect there to be important linkages in distribution and marketing and important executive expertise in how to maximize the performance of these similar businesses. Possibly the prepared meals business would be better sold to an FBC that is focusing on frozen food products or set up as an independent company.

A second FBC might be created from the two specialty retailing businesses. It is possible that executive expertise could be built up around how to run specialty retailing formats. There would also be synergy in the types of property and types of customer those businesses have. The grocery business, particularly if it is a middle-market or down-market business, should be sold or broken off.

In the hotels division, the picture is less clear. Some diversified hotel companies, like Forte was, are overdiversified and need to be broken up. Others, like Marriott, are FBCs and able to add more value than they subtract. (This does not mean that Marriott should retain all of its current businesses. But the bulk of its portfolio appears to be an FBC.) The answer, whether the hotel division is an FBC or an MBC, would depend on the plans, skills, and resources of the hotel division management team. If they had a strong argument, backed with good anecdotal or performance-based evidence, that they could add more value than they subtract, the division should be broken off as one FBC. If not, it should be broken into three separate businesses, some of which would be sold to other hotel-based FBCs.

It is worth emphasizing the logic we are using for the hotels division. The value destruction logic argues that we should break the division up into three businesses unless there is a strong rationale for not doing so. Our starting position is to prefer having businesses as independent companies, unless there are good reasons not to. This is the main message of this chapter. Without a strong rationale for value creation, our experience is that the net is usually negative. This is a radical message for most managers. Most argue from the other direction. "Without a strong logic for separation, we should stay together," they reason. And it sounds logical. But the value destruction is pervasive, as we have described here; it is real; and, with the rise of breakups, it is now being recognized.

To return to the Food and Hotel Corporation, if we assume that the hotel division is one FBC, we can decide how the company should be broken up. It should create three new FBCs—Food Manufacturing, Inc., Specialty Food Retailing, Inc., and Hotels, Inc. It should sell its two other businesses to corporate buyers or MBO teams—prepared foods and grocery retailing.

The breakup of Food and Hotel Corporation is driven by value destruction. Because it is a fictitious example, we cannot provide the anecdotes and analyses that prove the existence of value destruction. We must take for granted that the forces described here are at work in Food and Hotel Corporation. With no counterweight of value creation, breakup is inevitable.

The FBCs that emerge (Food Manufacturing, Inc., etc.) will still have the forces of value destruction. But their focus, assuming the logic we have provided is sound, will be sufficient to generate the counterweight: to generate a center with the skills to create value.

We are often asked why it is necessary to break up a company to create this focus. "If we decentralize effectively to the division levels, wouldn't we get value creation at those levels and eliminate any value destruction emanating from the corporate center?" If only this could be achieved. If only the solution was this easy. Unfortunately, the forces of value destruction are ingrained in the MBC model. Decentralization can reduce them, but it rarely reduces them enough to make the net positive.

Chapter 4

Do You Need to Break Up?

Don't wait until the heat is on. Look at breakup in a deliberate,
methodical way before trouble starts.

Breakup can no longer be pushed under the boardroom carpet.

Most large companies are overdiversified. Even after a decade of downsizing, Leveraged Buyouts (LBOs), divestment, and efforts to return to the core, most companies have portfolios that do not make sense. Managers have shed the obvious, cast off the orphans, and split up the warring teams. Yet there are still many companies that should have breakup on the agenda. In fact, by our estimate (see the Breakup 100 in the Appendix), between 58 percent and 66 percent of companies should be actively considering breakup. Is your company one of these? Do you need to place breakup at the top of your agenda?

This is a question that can no longer be pushed under the boardroom carpet. As of now, few boards view breakup as their favorite option. But in today's competitive environment, fewer can avoid putting it on the list of strategy options.

The Breakup 100 provides an externally based indication of whether a company is a candidate for breakup. In this chapter we take the analysis to the next level of detail. We lay out a method for managers to review their current situation and decide whether breakup should be at the top or the bottom of their list of options. The review will not resolve the breakup question itself. A final decision will depend on many detailed specifics, such as costs of separation, sale or flotation, the state of the market, and management's ability to develop a convincing logic for keeping the businesses together.

The review helps bring objectivity to these deliberations. It brings cold facts to the table that will either confirm the soundness of the current portfolio or encourage managers at the center to ask themselves the most searching questions about their role and the rationale for the existing portfolio.

A framework for conducting a corporate strategy review is described in a recent book, *Corporate-Level Strategy—Creating Value in the Multibusiness Company.* (Michael Goold, Andrew Campbell, and Marcus Alexander, John Wiley, 1994)

We now present an abridged version of this approach. It involves addressing four questions.

We should acknowledge that answering these questions takes courage. Men with pains in their chest often avoid doctors so as to avoid having to hear bad news. Sometime it's tough to take that first step. But the sooner the diagnosis is made, the quicker the patient can take remedial action—or get back to work, secure in the knowledge of confirmed good health.

QUESTION 1: WHAT ARE THE NATURAL CLUSTERS IN THE PORTFOLIO?

In Chapter 3, we looked at a model multibusiness company, the Hotel and Food Corporation. We concluded that the portfolio contained two or three natural "clusters"—manufacturing, specialty retailing, and possibly hotels—which could form the basis of focused business companies. We also identified two probable "odd-men-out"—prepared frozen meals, and grocery retailing. This section shows how the analysis is done.

Some managers find this question easy to answer. When asked to define the natural clusters, they will find no difficulty in listing those that fit well together, those that are odd-men-out, and those they are uncertain how to score. If you are in this position, fine—don't spend too long on the analyses we describe. The analyses are to help the undecided, to articulate the logic underlying the intuitive judgments, and to organize information for helping managers answer the second, much harder, question: whether the natural clusters are a good fit with the corporate center.

A good place to start is with the current divisions or groupings. Assuming the company is organized into divisions, these are likely to be the natural clusters. We are not suggesting any very fine-grained analysis. Cluster analysis involves taking the current portfolio of businesses and grouping them into ones that fit well together. If the portfolio is highly diverse, like General Electric, all the aerospace businesses may be put in one cluster, the consumer manufacturing businesses in another, etc. If the portfolio is tightly defined, it is still valuable to group it in clusters. For example, if the portfolio consists only of detergent businesses in different countries, then the European businesses would likely be in one cluster and the Asian businesses in another.

Clusters are defined by thinking about, first, value destruction and, second, value creation. Value destruction, we have argued, is an endemic part of the multibusiness company model. It comes from a lack of understanding by center managers of the details of individual businesses. Value destruction is reduced to a minimum, therefore, when the businesses are similar, when understanding the details of one business gives an understanding of all the businesses. Value destruction intensifies when the details are different, particularly the important details. What sort of details are we talking about? We are referring to the economics of the business, the needs of the customers, the technologies, supplies, culture, skills, advertising philosophies, pricing structures, and competitors.

Consider banking. Community banks such as Banc One or Nations Bank clearly contain similar businesses. Community banks in different towns or different states all serve similar customers. They all offer similar ranges of products. They all have similar back office functions. But the credit card business, the mortgage lending business, and the data processing businesses of these banks are less similar. They are different from the community banks and different from each other. The data processing business is one example. It has different economics, customers, technologies, suppliers, culture, skills, advertising, pricing, and more. Where businesses are as different as data processing and community banking, they do not belong in the same cluster.

It is harder, however, to judge a consumer finance business. It has different economics, similar customers, different technologies (e.g., database marketing), some similar suppliers (e.g., wholesale banks), and some similar competitors. The rule, however, is: if in doubt, leave it out. If not confident that a business fits in a particular cluster, then it doesn't.

The potential for value creation is the other side of the cluster equation. Value creation is about "opportunities for improvement" that depend on membership of the cluster. As we spelled out in Chapter 3, value creation can come from executive influence, linkage initiatives, central staffs, or portfolio development. Value creation depends on the center's expertise or resources. If the businesses need help the center can provide, there is an opportunity for improvement. If the center knows something commercially important that the businesses don't know, or if the center has some resource (e.g., a brand name or a patent license) that is valuable to the businesses, there are likewise opportunities for improvement. Where these opportunities for improvement are similar, a natural cluster exists: where they are different, the businesses are odd-men-out or should be in different clusters.

The final clustering, therefore, is based on a mix of two elements:

1. How similar are the *critical success factors* of the businesses and, hence, how easy will it be to avoid value destruction?

2. How similar are the *improvement opportunities,* and, hence, how easy will it be to develop the skills and resources to exploit them?

Separate analyses are needed to address these two questions.

Critical Success Factor Analysis

In every business, there are a few things that must be done really well. These are the things that distinguish good competitors from less good competitors.

Success may depend on the ability to develop new products. It may depend on service levels. It may depend on tight cost control or unique processing technology. Critical success factors are things a company must do well to be competitive.

In house building, for example, the critical success factors would be:

knowledge of the local market to help managers buy the right plot of land at a reasonable price and decide what type of house will sell best on that plot

speed of building the houses, to lower the holding cost of land and the overall cost of developing the site

purchasing skills and volumes to keep the cost of materials down

selling skills to ensure that houses are quickly sold at appropriate prices

In luxury perfume manufacturing the critical success factors are:

knowledge of the tastes, preferences, frailties, hopes, and moods of perfume buyers to help managers develop new fragrances and position them accurately

skill at marketing an image through name, packaging, advertising, and merchandising

the possession of a globally accepted, high-style brand name

established worldwide distribution channels through wholesalers, distributors, and retailers

It does not require a consultant from McKinsey and Company to conclude that house building and luxury perfume manufacture are not part of a natural cluster. The skills, values, and ambitions of the managers at each business are likely to be very different. They would be awkward participants in a common management meeting or corporate strategy session. They would be out of their depth if promoted to the corporate level and asked to take responsibility for the other business. Their mental maps, commercial rules of thumb, judgments about customers, suppliers, and staff would be inappropriate for the other business. It is a sure bet that bringing them together in a common cluster would result in value destruction.

By contrast, if we match the house building company with a similar business in another part of the country, these obviously belong in the same cluster. The mental maps, commercial values, rules of thumb, and judgments about people will be similar. Likewise, if we match the luxury perfume business with a luxury handbag business or a premium cosmetics business, we could expect a reasonable degree of fit.

How can we bring critical success factor analysis to bear on clustering? The process is to list, for each operating business in the portfolio, four to seven critical success factors. These can then be plotted on a chart (see Figure 19). The chart can be used to identify natural clusters of businesses with similar critical success factors, and businesses that don't fit easily in any of the clusters—odd-men-out. Don't force fit. In Figure 19 it is clear that there

FIGURE 19
Critical Success Factor Analysis

Critical success factors	Business					
	A	B	C	D	E	F
Product branding	✓					✓
Selling	✓					✓
Product mix management	✓					
Scale and capacity utilization	✓					
Business development skills		✓				
Formula branding			✓	✓	✓	
Positioning to match locality			✓	●	✓	
Site selection			●	✓	✓	✓
Property development costs			●	✓		✓
Value engineering			✓	✓		●
Detailed operating controls			✓	✓	✓	✓
Management selection and training			✓	✓	✓	✓
Supply chain logistics	✓		✓	✓	✓	✓
Low overheads	✓	✓	✓	✓	✓	✓

✓ critical factor   ● less important factor

is one cluster, embracing businesses, C, D, and E. The other businesses, A, B, and F, are odd-men-out.

Figure 20 provides another example. Although all these businesses are in the same industry—the construction industry—they do not form any natural clusters. House building, quarrying, and contracting do not fit naturally together.

Critical success factor analysis raises two important issues. First, how do we choose which factors to record? Businesses normally have to do many things well to succeed. The answer has to be a matter of judgment. There is no science. The judgments we are trying to make are: Which factors are critical in distinguishing successful from less successful businesses? Among competitors with similar strategies in the same product/market areas, what distinguishes the good from the less good?

The second issue concerns businesses that contain subunits with very different critical success factors—a branded-food business that also does contract manufacturing, a restaurant that also does take-out food, an airline that

FIGURE 20

Critical Success Factor Analysis: Building Industry

Critical success factors	Business		
	Quarrying	Construction	Housing
Chosing the "right" contracts		✓	
Efficient project management		✓	
Profit-focused culture		✓	
Effective financial accounting		✓	
Knowing the local market			✓
Buying land at the "right" time			✓
Efficient building system			✓
Marketing and selling skills			✓
Location of quarry	✓		
Service to key customers	✓		
Decisions about new equipment	✓		
Maintaining stable prices	✓		

also does charter flights. Situations like this are common and can create real dilemmas. The bias should be to treat the different activity as another business and record its critical success factors separately. However, ignore the general rule ("if in doubt leave it out") if the activity is:

an integral part of the main business
small in relation to the main business, and
hard to separate into an independent business.

Using these criteria on the examples above, take-out food would be considered part of the restaurant business, whereas both contract manufacturing and charter flights could and probably should be separated and analyzed in their own right.

Improvement Opportunity Analysis

The corporate center can only add value if there are opportunities to improve the performance of the businesses. Another dimension of natural clusters is therefore the similarity that exists in the nature of the improvement opportunities. The analysis involves specifying what the improvement opportunities are in each business and creating clusters of businesses around similar improvement opportunities.

The reason for creating clusters around improvement opportunities is evident. If the corporate center has a group of businesses with the same improvement opportunities, the corporate center's job is easier: it has a better chance of adding substantial amounts of value. Think of the center as a doctor. If all the doctor's patients have similar health problems, it is easier for the doctor to carry out an accurate diagnosis and develop specialist medicines for the particular health problem. But if the doctor is faced with a different health problem every day, he or she cannot develop specialist expertise. Each new patient is a new challenge requiring new knowledge and new treatment.

Improvement opportunities exist in all shapes and sizes. Businesses can have opportunities to grow faster. The opportunity may be about finding ways to enter adjacent markets, develop new product or service features, improve the impact of advertising, raise the quality of marketing, or motivate the sales force differently. Businesses can have opportunities to raise prices. The opportunity may be in setting different pricing strategies for separate customer groups, changing pricing structures for added features, or changing pricing for different occasions, times of the year, or points in the industry cycle. Businesses can have opportunities to lower costs. The opportunities may be about finding ways to cut overhead, improve productivity, reduce the price of supplies, or reduce levels of working capital. The list of potential areas of improvement opportunities is long.

Figure 21 provides a step-by-step process for defining improvement opportunities starting from the business units' existing plans. This process assumes that the business plan is well formulated. If it is not, if the strategies of one or more of the businesses need review, a more rigorous process is necessary. This process should start with the development of a sound, potential-maximizing plan for each business. These plans then form the foundations on which the improvement opportunity analysis is built.

The business plan lists the major tasks that the unit will tackle in the next few years. For a drugstore retailer, the tasks might be:

FIGURE 21
Identifying Improvement Opportunities

1.	List, for each business, the 4–7 major tasks facing the management team. Consider whether they are likely to underperform in any of these tasks. If so, there is an improvement opportunity.
2.	Use the improvement opportunity check list (illustration 22) to generate additional ideas about improvement opportunities.
3.	List the typical mistakes that managers make in this industry. Each typical mistake is a potential improvement opportunity.
4.	Examine the center's current activities—executive influence, linkage initiatives, central staff, and portfolio development. Decide what influence the center is having on the businesses. Consider whether this influence is addressing an improvement opportunity.
5.	Consider the MBCs and FBCs that own similar businesses. What improvement opportunities are they addressing?

double the number of stores with pharmacies

convert 200 stores to the new health and beauty format

convert 100 stores to the household and drug format

raise employee commitment and morale

reengineer supply-chain management to reduce stock-outs and lower
supply costs.

Business plans have many action items, but it is usually possible to define four to seven major tasks—the ones that will have a large impact on future success.

Armed with a list of these tasks, the analysis asks an important question. Is there any reason to suppose that the business's management team will underperform in any of these tasks? If so, which tasks and why? Let us suppose we have asked this question of the drugstore business unit and got the following answer. Managers of the unit are likely to underperform in:

Improving employee commitment and morale because:

management's current style is part of the problem

managers have already made one attempt and failed

management is not aware of the latest change-management techniques or
the best consultants.

Changing supply-chain management because:

the current VP for supply-chain management is not viewed as part of the
top team and therefore fails to carry sufficient weight on cross-functional
issues

the president's marketing philosophy is "pile-it-high, sell-it-cheap," and
he does not understand the latest thinking in supply management

the whole team underestimates the size of the task.

These two areas—improving employee morale and reengineering the supply-chain—are improvement opportunities. If the corporate center has the appropriate skills and resources, it will be able to add substantial amounts of value to this business.

For most businesses, the process of defining tasks and identifying causes of likely underperformance is the best way to uncover improvement opportunities. But improvement opportunities can also be identified in four other ways.

1. Figure 22 provides a list of areas where businesses often underperform. If any of these items are relevant to the business unit, they may point to additional improvement opportunities. For example, the drugstore unit may be overlooking a business-definition issue—the health and beauty store

FIGURE 22
Improvement Opportunities Check List

1.	*Business Definition*. Is the business defined so as to maximize its sources of competitive advantage?
2.	*Business Size*. Does the business suffer from problems related to being small (e.g. management succession, financial control skills) or big (e.g. bureaucracy, loss of motivation)?
3.	*Management*. Does the business have top quality managers relative to its competitors? Are its managers focused on the right objectives/ambitions? Is the business dependent on attracting and retaining unusual people?
4.	*Temptations*. Does the business encourage managers to make mistakes (e.g. maturity often leads to excessive diversification; long product cycles can lead to excessive reliance on old products; cyclical swings can lead to too much investment during the upswing)?
5.	*Linkages*. Could this business effectively link with other businesses to improve efficiency or market position? Are the linkages complex or difficult to establish between the units concerned?
6.	*Common Capabilities*. Does this business have capabilities in common with other businesses that could be built, shared, and transferred between the businesses?
7.	*Special Expertise*. Could this business benefit from specialist or rare expertise that the parent possesses or could possess?
8.	*External Relations*. Does this business have difficult-to-manage external stakeholders (shareholders, government, unions, suppliers, etc.) that could be better managed by the parent company?
9.	*Major Decisions*. Does the business face difficult and infrequent decisions in which it lacks expertise (entry into China, major acquisitions, major capacity extensions)? Would it be difficult to get funding for major investments from external providers?
10.	*Major Change*. Is the business facing a need to make major changes for which its management has insufficient experience?

concept is evolving into a different business from the household and drug-store concept: the management team needs to separate these two concepts more fully.

Or it may be failing to work closely enough with a sister unit involved in gro-cery retailing on issues such as common purchasing and shared distribution.

Both of these are additional improvement opportunities that can be ad-dressed by a corporate center with the right skills.

2. Another way of identifying improvement opportunities is to think about typical mistakes that managers make in some industries. For example, in the office furniture market, niche businesses frequently make the mistake of overdiversifying. A business specializing in cheap swivel chairs expands into midrange swivel chairs or desks or tables. Because there are few economies of scale, because these niche players are competing against full-range suppliers, and because design skills are specialized, attempts to diver-sify out of a niche often create problems. This is an improvement opportunity: a center can create value—or, more accurately, prevent the de-struction of value—by stopping its businesses from making this mistake.

3. A third way of identifying improvement opportunities is to examine the executive influence, linkage initiatives, and central staffs of the center. What impact are these having on the businesses? Is the impact positive? If so, what is the reason? What is the improvement opportunity? One company had a central staff that built factories for the business units. Because the com-pany was expanding in many less-developed countries and because most of the factories were producing similar products, the factory-building team added value. Each business unit might only build one factory every five years; the central team built five or more each year. Moreover, because the central team specialized in one type of factory, they were better than outside contractors at their specialization. Factory construction was an improvement opportunity for those businesses with plans to build factories.

4. The final way of identifying improvement opportunities is to look at what other corporate centers are doing with their businesses. Other compa-

nies that own similar businesses may have identified different improvement opportunities. By observing what they are doing, it is often possible for alert managers to learn from the improvement opportunities their rivals have spotted. Hanson led the world in spotting the opportunity to cut the fat out of mature businesses with strong market positions. Hanson managers discovered that these cash-cow businesses could be run at even higher levels of profitability than other managers realized. Gradually, other managers began copying Hanson, until there were many corporate centers chasing the same deals—and many managers of underperforming companies putting their houses in order to fend off a possible takeover. The final ironic result has been the breakup of Hanson. The improvement opportunity dried up and corporate Hanson could not find another way of creating value.

Figure 22 is a quick guide to improvement opportunity analysis. Each step will yield, for each business, a list (sometimes a long one) of improvement opportunities. For the list to be useful, it needs to be quantified. Is the improvement opportunity worth $100 million or $10 million? Will it improve return on sales by 0.1 percent or 1.0 percent?

The next step is to cluster businesses by the similarity of the improvement opportunities. Focus on the big opportunities. Different clusters will stand out. One cluster may need help with international expansion. Another cluster may need to upgrade its purchasing and supply-chain management. For a third cluster, the common requirement may be to set stretching cash flow targets.

Refining the Clusters

Cluster analysis is not a science, and it's not meant to be. The objective is to take the current portfolio and sort the current businesses into clusters that make sense. The objective is to define "natural" clusters, groups of businesses with similar critical success factors and similar improvement opportunities. Sometimes the natural clusters are clear. More normally there are shades of gray. The central point of one cluster may be clearly distinct from the central point of another, for example a community banking cluster versus a corporate banking cluster. But the edges will be blurred and businesses in the middle could be placed in either cluster or treated as an odd-man-out.

Our advice is pragmatic rather than scientific. Push the cluster analysis as hard as seems appropriate. Don't be satisfied with concluding that there is just one cluster; try pushing to a greater level of detail. Be suspicious of very large clusters. Try breaking them up into subclusters. Be suspicious of differences, always looking to see if differences should result in different cluster definitions. However, be equally suspicious if the analysis results in concluding that every business is its own cluster (i.e., there are no clusters). If every business is different in some way from every other, start looking for similarities and forming clusters around these similarities.

The bad news of cluster analysis is that there are many shades of gray: it can be easy to argue different points of view. The good news is that, in our experience, managers normally agree on 90 percent of the clustering decisions. Disagreements about the remaining 10 percent can be important and should be recorded for further debate. But the first step is to get 90 percent of the portfolio arranged into clusters and odd-men-out.

The purpose of cluster analysis is to try to identify those groups of businesses that are highly likely to form the portfolio of a focused business company: similar critical success factors and similar improvement opportunities. The purpose of cluster analysis is to take a multibusiness company portfolio and group the businesses into clusters that would clearly make sense as focused business companies.

In other chapters we have talked about Multibusiness Companies (MBCs) and Focused Business Companies (FBCs). In the light of our cluster analysis we can now revisit these definitions. An FBC is a company that owns businesses with similar critical success factors and similar improvement opportunities. In an FBC, the center can develop specialized skills for addressing the opportunities and so add value. In an FBC the center can understand the businesses well enough not to destroy value (at least not so much that the net is negative). An FBC is, therefore, an MBC with a portfolio of businesses well enough focused to make breakup undesirable. An FBC could also be called an FMBC, a Focused Multibusiness Company.

Discovering that your portfolio contains more than one cluster does not necessarily put breakup on the agenda. Remember that the clustering was not done as a scientific exercise. Also the clustering process encouraged you to look for more than one cluster, even if all of the businesses are fairly similar.

You need to address the rest of the questions before you can decide whether to put breakup on the agenda.

QUESTION 2: DOES THE CENTER FIT WITH THE CLUSTER OR CLUSTERS?

The second question builds on the answer to the first. With an understanding about the critical success factors and, more importantly, the improvement opportunities of each cluster, we can decide whether the cluster fits with the center. Does the center have the skills and resources needed to address the improvement opportunities? How easy will it be for the center to develop the needed skills and resources? Does the center have a good understanding of businesses with these critical success factors? Does it understand them well enough to keep value destruction to a minimum?

These questions are not easy to answer. They are as hard to answer as questions about whether a particular manager will be good or bad at a particular task. They are nearly impossible to answer if the underlying assumption is that a good manager can manage anything. In fact, the questions only have meaning if you recognize, as we do, that management skills are specialized. This is a fundamental point that is often overlooked. At a corporate center some managers are good at understanding retail businesses, others are good at understanding specialty chemicals. Some managers are good at helping businesses with their international strategies, others are good at helping them coordinate distribution, and still others are good at helping them cut overhead and rationalize. But no one is good at everything.

Personal experience confirms this view. All of us have had bosses, colleagues, or subordinates who are good at some things and less good at others.

So should a good corporate center contain a variety of these skills? Should it have some managers who understand retailing and others who understand specialty chemicals, some who can help businesses internationalize and others who can help businesses rationalize? The answer is no.

First, managers with the required corporate center skills are rare. They are not freely available on the market. If they were, the improvement opportunity wouldn't exist in the first place. The business would already be improved. The reason there is an opportunity is precisely that the business is attempting to achieve something that requires skills that are not readily available. So the idea of packing the center with all the skills and resources necessary to support all the clusters is naive.

Second, managers with different skill sets don't fit easily together, especially in a small corporate center. The center needs to make a choice between skills that don't fit well together. Rationalizers usually have different beliefs and values from business builders. Retailers have different beliefs and values from chemical engineers. Commodity chemical engineers even have different beliefs and values from specialty chemical engineers. If different types of managers work together in a small corporate center, there will inevitably be disagreements about management style and philosophy. Alternatively, a compromise culture will grow up that is less effective for both sets of managers.

This discussion of management skills underlines how hard it is to decide whether the clusters fit well with the center or not. The fit judgment depends on the assessment of what the center is good and bad at; what it could become good at and what it is likely to remain bad at. These decisions are not easy, especially for the CEO. It is hard for the top managers to admit that they are not good at rationalizing businesses, that they do not fully understand retailing, or that they are creating a culture that inhibits the internationalization of their businesses. The temptation is to give themselves the benefit of the doubt.

Objective data to counter this subjectivity are scarce, but some are available. The most valuable simply document the personal track record. This does not mean that managers are condemned to repeat their past successes or failures. It does mean that, at 55 years old or even earlier, managers find it hard to learn new skills that rub up against well-grooved weaknesses. When looking at the track record, therefore, look for signs of ingrained weaknesses. These are pointers to management behaviors that are hardest to change.

Successes and Failures Analysis

Successes and failures analysis is a good way to identify these well-grooved weaknesses. Identify a list of major decisions over the last five or ten years (the tenure of the current center management team) and score them success, failure, or undecided. Initiatives might include:

acquisitions
new product launches
major investments
important appointments
culture change efforts
corporate reorganizations.

Scoring these initiatives will produce a profile of the things that the company, under the influence of this central management team, has done well, and, more particularly, what it has done badly.

Opinions of Business Managers

Opinions of business managers are another source of data that is external to the views of the cluster itself. Business managers are the "customers" of the "help" that the center gives. They normally have strong views about the center's strengths and weaknesses. Their opinions should be sought as assiduously as those of any other customer.

But business-level managers are biased too. Their views are not the gospel. A combination of self-analysis by corporate-center managers, "customer" evaluation by business-level managers, and track record based on successes and failures analysis normally generates a realistic assessment of the center's character and special abilities.

We would not, however, advise a written strengths and weaknesses profile of the center. Putting strengths and weaknesses down on paper creates the wrong dynamic. Intuition and instinct are apt to lose out to wordsmithing and politics.

Instead of a strengths and weaknesses profile, get the different groups of managers to capture their opinions in the form of a "fit judgment." Ask center managers which clusters fit best and which fit badly. Ask business managers the same question. If those who have carried out the successes and failures analysis are different, ask them too. It is likely that there will be comparatively little disagreement. The main dissension will come from those who think that good managers can manage anything. We believe that their views should be discounted.

At this stage in the analysis, disagreements should be exposed to discussion and debate, but not resolution. If the CEO says his or her skills fit, no ambitious center manager is apt to disagree too strongly. The purpose of the debate should be to clarify views, not finalize judgments. Two more questions need to be answered before final decisions are reached.

QUESTION 3: IS THERE A LOGIC FOR KEEPING THE CLUSTERS TOGETHER?

Question 2 was about which clusters fit best with the center and which fit worst. Question 3 concerns strategy. Do the corporate managers at the center have a logic for keeping the clusters together? In other words, can managers convincingly argue that their company, combining two or more of the clusters, can become and remain an FBC?

Is there a good reason why the center can and should focus on more than one cluster? Why would it not be better to break up the group and focus on the cluster that fits best with the center? Why not have the center managers focus on what they are best at? Why not specialize in the qualities appropriate to one and leave other management teams to focus on the others?

If today's justifications for a multicluster portfolio include any of the following, breakup should be on the agenda:

"If we broke up, the group would be too small."
"We need more clusters to provide more growth opportunities."
"We don't want to have all our eggs in one basket."

"We are good at *x*, but the future lies with *y*, therefore we must be in *y* as well."

"We need balance in our portfolio. Cluster *x* is cash hungry. We need some stability as well."

"Cluster *x* is cyclical. With more clusters we can produce higher 'quality' earnings."

"The shareholders invested in us because we are broadly spread, hence we should not focus too much."

Although surprisingly common, these are not just weak justifications for diversification; they are likely to lead to value destruction. Managers with these thoughts in their heads are a dangerous influence on decision making. They are likely to encourage their company to diversify into businesses it can add nothing to. The premiums paid will not be offset by improvements and the MBC created will start destroying value.

These thoughts are often deeply ingrained. Many managers have been taught to believe in balance, risk spreading, growth at all costs, and so on. Their beliefs are not based on self-promotion. They sincerely believe these are good ways to think. They may be reinforced by thoughts of self-preservation, but more normally managers believe that the above ideas are right. Today's old-style MBCs would not exist if they didn't. Tomorrow's multicluster FBCs need to be built on better logic.

If the common rationales for multicluster businesses are wrong, what are the right ones? Rationales that underpin major value creation and minimal value destruction. Value creation is highest when improvement opportunities and critical success factors are similar across clusters. This makes it possible for the center to become expert at the improvement opportunities and develop an instinctive feel for those things that are important to its businesses.

Value destruction is lowest when the critical success factors are similar (reducing the chance of inappropriate policies or interventions) and the degree of autonomy is high (reducing the number of areas where businesses need to seek guidance).

Rationales for multicluster FBCs need to be examined closely. Procter and Gamble and Unilever are examples. They have clusters of businesses in detergents, in household cleaning products, in personal products like toothpaste, in food, and in some other fast-moving consumer goods. The critical success factors of these mass-market, fast-moving, brand-oriented consumer goods are fairly similar. The improvement opportunities—linking other businesses in different countries, centralizing research and development, mass-marketing skills—are also fairly similar. Their multicluster portfolios (with some exceptions) make sense. They have a rationale that works.

Does this mean that Procter and Gamble and Unilever have only one cluster? Does this mean that detergents and household cleaning products are really part of one cluster? The answer is yes and no. Detergents and household cleaning products appear to be similar enough to be part of an FBC. But in portfolios that contain large numbers of these businesses, they would clearly be categorized into different clusters, raising the question of whether they should be broken apart (i.e., whether they would perform better as separate, more highly focused FBCs). In fact, detergents and household cleaning products may well be sufficiently different that they would be better off in separate FBCs. Clorox is a US company focused mainly on household cleaning products and has been gaining ground on Procter and Gamble. Reckitt and Colman is another successful company that has decided to focus primarily on household cleaning. If this more focused strategy proves successful, the pressure on Procter and Gamble or Unilever to break off their household cleaning activities will increase.

The purpose of this detergent and household cleaning example is to point out that there are no absolutes, and that the situation is changing. To go forward confidently with a multicluster portfolio management needs to have a strong logic for keeping the businesses together.

To justify highly diverse multicluster portfolios like those of KKR (Kholberg, Kravis and Roberts) or Virgin requires even more convincing rationales. In these companies the center adds value by focusing on a narrow set of corporate-level skills, and avoids destroying value by insisting on high degrees of decentralization.

KKR is an investment firm that owns controlling stakes in about twenty-five companies, with total sales of more than $30 billion. De facto, KKR is one of America's largest diversified companies. KKR has clusters in food and publishing, and quite a few odd-men-out.

KKR creates value by deal-making, financial engineering, raising money, and motivating managers using equity and debt. At the same time, it avoids value destruction by decentralization. Many of KKR's businesses are publicly quoted, forcing them to think and act independently of KKR's influence. All of them have external directors who bring independent views to boardroom discussions, thus diluting KKR's influence. In addition KKR reduces further the risk of overinfluencing its businesses by exerting its influence through the broad structure, rather than through one-to-one relationships.

Virgin, the creation of the exuberant Richard Branson, is another example. Virgin is even more diverse than KKR, but equally successful. Branson took his company private in 1988 for £248 million. Today it is reputed to be worth more than £1 billion ($1.6 billion).

Virgin has a travel and tourism cluster, a media cluster, a retailing cluster, a consumer products cluster, and a financial services cluster.

Branson creates extra value by letting these businesses use the Virgin brand. Through his personality, his talent for publicity, and his unconventional, antiestablishment image, Branson has created a unique brand position. The Virgin brand stands for fun, for unstuffiness, for championing the consumer, for taking on the establishment. Branson looks for business propositions that fit this mold. His staff screens twenty propositions a week. Virgin invests in fewer than twenty a year.

Branson avoids value destruction with a unique philosophy of decentralized management by visibly demonstrating his commitment not to interfere, a commitment that was symbolically reinforced for many years by having his corporate center on a barge on a canal in London. Decentralization is backed up by the award of large stakes in many of the companies to managers and other investors. As with KKR, outside investment helps to dilute the risk of his influence being negative. Once an investment has been made, Virgin is more of an investor than a corporate center. Indeed, outsiders trying to understand the company as a conventional corporation are regularly confused by the absence of anything resembling an organization chart. The major difference with KKR is that Branson needs to keep tight control over how the Virgin brand is used.

Both KKR and Virgin manage to be highly diversified and yet pass the multicluster test. Not many other companies can boast the same. Those that do normally have very similar clusters. For instance, Johnson & Johnson and Hewlett-Packard have many clusters; but most of them are very similar in both critical success factors and improvement opportunities.

Much the same applies to 3M, another famously diverse FBC, especially since the recent refocusing of its portfolio. In 1995, 3M broke off its alien clusters in tape and imaging products. It retained the businesses where 3M's unique dedication to technical superiority, research and development, and small decentralized units is appropriate.

3M creates value by pushing its businesses to innovate, with aggressive sales targets, such as 40 percent of sales from products launched in the last three years, and profit targets often as high as 25 percent return on sales.

3M avoids value destruction through its special brand of decentralized management, where technical directors are expected to be the champions of their businesses and where all business initiatives are sponsored from the bottom up.

Precisely because they are so extreme, KKR, Virgin, and 3M strikingly demonstrate the combination of qualities that must be present to justify a multicluster strategy. There must be some improvement opportunities that are common to all clusters, there must be some skills at the center that seek out and address these opportunities, and there must be a management philosophy of decentralization to minimize the risk of value destruction.

QUESTION 4: DOES THE MULTICLUSTER LOGIC STAND UP TO CHALLENGE?

If managers are proposing a multicluster strategy, deep questioning is required to test the logic. Where and how is the value to be created? What justification is there for thinking they can avoid value destruction? Are central managers fooling themselves in the assessment of their own skills or the fit with the improvement opportunities?

The final question is therefore aimed at uncovering wishful thinking. A multicluster strategy must withstand three challenges:

Will investors buy it?

Does past performance support it?

What hard evidence can be provided?

Exhibit 2

IS THERE A LOGIC FOR GE?

And now a word about General Electric. We are often asked whether GE is not such a major exception to our way of thinking about value destruction and corporate breakups as to cast doubt on our whole framework. After all, it is huge, highly diversified, and yet very successful. How do we explain this?

We cannot of course prove that GE should break up. That would require an analysis of the sort we are describing in this chapter. The question is: should breakup be on GE's agenda?

To leave GE as it is, we would need to argue that GE is in an FBC: that it is built around some powerful corporate center skills. And these skills must add 10 percent or more to the value of the business. Because GE is so diverse (aircraft engines, financial services, television broadcasting, appliances, chemicals, etc.), the burden of proof should be with management. GE needs to convince us that it is an FBC.

This is what Jack Welch tried to do in his 1995 annual report. "Breaking up is the right answer for some big companies. For us it is the wrong answer," he comments and then goes on to explain why he believes the corporate center adds enough value to warrant staying together. The text, which takes up the

---

(continued)

whole of his ten-page letter to shareholders, is persuasive. Welch argues that the center's contribution in his first five years was the portfolio restructuring to concentrate on leadership businesses: he drove all of GE's businesses onward or outward; either they had to be first or second in their respective markets or they were out. In the next five years, the center set about delayering and improving management processes, using the "workout" approach, with widespread managerial involvement in continuous improvement. In the past five years the focus has been on eliminating boundaries everywhere, both within the company and with those it deals with on the outside.

Moreover, Welch has a track record that suggests that the net influence is positive. While we are believers in the benefits of breakup and are skeptical of the ability of any manager to cope with such diversity, we give GE the benefit of the doubt. Welch's relentless pursuit of bureaucracy, his insistence on globalization, his passion for best practice, his commitment to boundlessness, and his readiness to explain what he is doing may be sufficient to justify GE today.

Looking ahead, however, particularly at a GE without Jack Welch, we predict breakup. Not only will the benefits of bureaucracy busting and boundlessness have run their course, but GE will be unlikely to find someone with the same clarity of vision and leadership skills. When the breakup comes, we see financial services and RCA/NBC as separate spin-offs, leaving GE with its core manufacturing businesses.

Will Investors Buy It?

How will investors react to the proposed strategy? If the strategy is no change, the assessment is easy. We can rely on current commentary among analysts and journalists. Are they calling for breakup or lauding management for the quality of its strategic thinking?

Look at the shareholders' verdict. If the company is worth more than the breakup value of its businesses, shareholders implicitly believe that management is worth a premium for its strategic thinking. If there is a value gap, and the company is worth less than its breakup value, the verdict is the reverse: far from being worth a premium, central management rates a discount. Its existence is destroying value compared to some alternative ownership structure.

We have been involved in many breakup valuations. They are not easy to do (see Figure 23). Some yield inconclusive results. But, more often than not, they point to a value gap. This is a challenge to the status quo that is difficult to sweep under the carpet.

If the strategy is new, and if it does not build on the past, the opinion of investors must be canvassed through presentations and discussions. From our experience, this is a risky step that should not be initiated until management is confident of its strategy. Even when management is confident, it should treat the reactions of investors with respect. Investors have seen the hard results of past corporate dreams and hopes. They can often distinguish

FIGURE 23
How to Do a Breakup Valuation

1. Use the current plans of each business to develop a valuation (using discounted cash flow [DCF] methods) of that business. Compare the total value, less the cost of the corporate center (also valued using DCF methods), less the company's debt, with the company's market capitalization.
   Choose a range of market capitalizations, over the last year. Give more weight to periods when the market's view of the future was closest to your company's planning assumptions.

2. Do the same analysis using the price/earnings ratio as the valuation technique. Each business should be valued on its current earnings using a price/earnings ratio of a suitable market peer group.

3. Estimate the sale value of any businesses that could be readily sold to other corporate buyers. Use recent transactions as a guide, but adjust these if the market conditions have changed substantially in the the meantime.

4. These valuation techniques may give significantly different answers. Broadly the guidelines are these:

   ☐ if the peer group valuations exceed the current market capitalization, the market thinks a breakup would be desirable; a breakup should be considered

   ☐ if the DCF analysis gives higher values than the others, the market does not understand (or believe) the prospects for your businesses; either the analysis is wrong or the market should be "resold"

   ☐ if sale valuations for particular businesses exceed P/E valuations, there are rivals who believe they can add value to these businesses; in these circumstances, a trade sale should be better than a spinoff sound ideas from foolish ones. On the one hand, they have the experience of the market behind them. On the other hand, they can be averse to risk: they may prefer to support a track record rather than a plan because they have little real understanding of business. Their reactions need to be read carefully.

Does Past Performance Support It?

Performance analysis is useful when the new strategy can be compared with similar strategies in the past. What evidence is there to prove this strategy succeeded before? Did the company or that part of the company outperform when it followed this strategy? Have other companies pursuing this strategy done well?

It is easy for managers to become emotionally committed to their ideas. Simple performance analysis often comes as a shock. Managers may see sales growing and profits rising, but overlook the fact that their company's figures are growing less fast than inflation, less fast than the average, or less fast than a suitable peer group.

Choosing the right indicators to compare performance with is an important part of the exercise. A peer group is an essential part of good performance analysis. Another important indicator is the cost of capital. Has the company or division earned more than its cost of capital?

Performance analysis can be carried out for the company as a whole to test the soundness of the historic strategy. It also can be performed on individual businesses.

The purpose of comparative performance at the business level is to assess whether the value the corporate center believes it is adding can be detected in business results. Are our business units doing better than independent businesses or businesses owned by more focused companies? If not, there is something wrong with the clusters, with the strategy, or with both.

We have noted the spectacular performance contrast between independent mineral companies and those owned by oil companies. The strategic planner of a famous leisure company, involved in a number of high-profile acquisitions, conceded to us that the company's businesses were performing worse than those of a peer group of good independents. These single business competitors were outperforming his company by 2 percent on return on sales and by 7 percent on return on assets. Despite this evidence of value destruction, the planner had not been able to slow down the rate of acquisition. "Growth ambitions have their own momentum," he commented, "and we seem to be doing fine at the moment." As we write, the company is still doing fine. But, as one would expect, we anticipate trouble.

What Hard Evidence Can Be Provided?

From years of assessing whether centers are creating value or not, we believe it is normally possible to collect hard evidence that will demonstrate the case one way or the other. The problem is not lack of evidence; it is that few companies put in enough effort to fully test their thinking.

If the company is building its strategy around internationalization, as many companies do, it should be possible to test the evidence. Look at previous attempts to internationalize the company's businesses. Document the stories. Who did what to whom? Whose idea was it? Who suggested that joint venture? Where did the commitment to Asia emerge from? What was the influence of the center? What actually happened?

As academics know, writing history is hard, but it is revealing. The company myth about the Asian strategy or the European disaster rarely matches the real story. Careful sifting of the evidence helps to avoid strategies built on myths.

In one company we were told that the corporate center had a rare ability to create a motivated culture with a family feel. The company had been able to acquire businesses at reasonable prices because they were attracted by the family culture. Moreover, the center was good at allowing the acquired businesses to maintain their own culture and encouraging managers to pursue more ambitious strategies. This logic has led the company to buy a range of businesses, developing them into three clusters and six odd-men-out.

When we talked to the company managers and previous owners, however, a rather different story emerged. The company, they argued, had paid generously, often too generously, for their businesses. The center managers, all from the original business, showed little cultural flexibility. Far from encouraging differences, they were liable to impose inappropriate policies on the acquired businesses. Managers in the new businesses were fearful of being swamped by the culture of the core business and constrained by the caution of the center.

Subsequently, a number of the senior business managers left—some to start businesses in competition with their old companies. Not long after that, the CEO retired early and the company is now rationalizing its portfolio.

GETTING BREAKUP ON THE AGENDA

For some companies, the implications of our four questions will be limited to disposing of businesses that are odd-men-out: rationalizing the portfolio. For most it will mean facing up to a more radical decision: breakup or at least breaking off one or more clusters.

Don't wait until the heat is on. Nearly every company we have observed has felt some sort of pressure to do something. But once the company is on the defensive, the process can be unnecessarily rushed and action can even be taken for the wrong reasons.

Our advice is to look at breakup in a deliberate, methodical, and objective way before trouble starts. Analysis of the kind we suggest above can be helpful in addressing a tough question in a controlled, professional way. Better it should produce results the management team accepts than to be taking action with a gun to management's head.

The value of getting breakup on the agenda early is that it allows time for proper consideration. Managers can be educated into thinking about value creation and value destruction, and hypotheses can be tested. Managers often take a long time to accept the force of our value destruction logic. They are uncomfortable about breaking up "just because the logic for staying together is weak." They want a positive logic for breaking up and need to be shown that the elimination of value destruction is a sound logic.

We have discussed breakup and its implications with many top managers. At some point they often say something like this:

> OK, I hear what you're saying and your logic is hard to fault. But I have to tell you that we are simply not ready to throw in the towel. There is just too much emotional commitment around here to this thing that we've built over all these years. After all, the wolf is not at the door; we're doing OK. There's no crisis. I really doubt I could get this through my board. *Isn't there some other way?*

We typically have three things to say at this stage.

First, we are realists and pragmatists and accept that it is often impossible for big organizations to embark on radical, disruptive exercises like this without severe external pressure. Without it, many organizations simply cannot muster the will to bite the bullet. We understand that. But such companies must recognize that, without a frontal assault on value destruction, they are forgoing a major wealth-creating opportunity and, in the long run, their days are numbered. The market will eventually catch up with them.

Second, there is a way for chief executives, undecided about the merits of breakup, to move forward. It is hard to take a revolutionary step like breakup when you are undecided about its merits. We, therefore, offer a more evolutionary process. This involves identifying the "cluster" in the portfolio that best fits with the corporate center and offers the most promise for the future. Normally this cluster is one that is large and "core," one that has been in the portfolio for many years. Sometimes, however, the chosen cluster may be small and new to the portfolio: selected because of its promise rather than it longevity.

Once a cluster has been selected, management should focus on developing an ambitious corporate strategy for this cluster. Sources of value creation need to be clearly identified; the center's skills and resources need to be defined; sources of value destruction need to be removed; and experience needs to be gained in implementing the strategy for this cluster, including any acquisitions that support the strategy.

With a clear sense of the corporate strategy that is appropriate for the chosen cluster, and an understanding of whether the strategy will meet management and shareholder expectations, the chief executive can now decide what to do with the rest of the portfolio. The delay between choosing a cluster to focus on and being confident of the strategy for this chosen cluster may be one, two, or three years. During this period the other businesses should be treated as valued members of the portfolio and encouraged to develop to their full. Once management feels confident of the chosen cluster, it then has a "core strategy" against which to evaluate the rest of the portfolio.

Odd-men-out businesses can probably be quickly dealt with. Either they fit with the core strategy or they don't. Clusters that are highly dissimilar can also be quickly judged. They need to be broken off or sold to a parent company that will fit better with their needs. The difficult decision, in this second phase of analysis, is what to do about clusters of businesses that are somewhat dissimilar.

The answer is to focus on developing corporate strategies for these clusters in the same way as for the core cluster. As these strategies develop, the future will become clear. The other clusters will either reinforce and support the core strategy, neatly fitting alongside, or awkwardly rub against it. Those that rub need to be broken off.

Third, the tone of this book suggests that this other way, this evolutionary way, this nonbreakup way, is not the preferred choice. One might expect us to pooh-pooh managers who decide not to break up because they are unconvinced of its merits or because they want to try harder to make sense of the portfolio they have. This book is clearly written in praise of breakup. We do believe that breakup is a highly positive strategy, which many more companies should pursue. But we also recognize that it is not the right way forward for all companies. We would like breakup to be seriously considered. But the more evolutionary solution is an alternative that some managers will prefer. So long as it addresses the objective of reducing value destruction and increasing value creation, who are we to complain?

Chapter 5

Anatomy of a Breakup

None of those who had been through the breakup process regret it or
believe the effort was wasted.

The breakup turbo-charged Lilly stock. Investors prefer to design their
own portfolios and thus we are now more attractive to them.

—Charles Schalliol, Eli Lilly

B reakup is a life-giving, wealth-creating phenomenon. But like so many
other good things, breaking up is hard to do. That message comes
through loud and clear from our study of twenty landmark breakups in the
US and ten in the UK. Though the technicalities are different in the two
countries, the managerial experiences are similar. They are traumatic. The
good news is that managers are overwhelmingly positive about breakups
they have experienced—if only after the event.

Chapter 5 describes what breakup is like: what the various stages in the
process are, how it feels, and the situations that appear to arise typically
along the way. It then goes on to draw some conclusions in the form of a list
of tips for successful breakup.

123

THE FOUR STAGES IN THE PROCESS

We have identified four stages in the typical breakup:

Stage 1: Pressure for breakup
Stage 2: Resistance and acquiescence
Stage 3: Breaking up
Stage 4: Rebirth

We trace each stage and illustrate it with examples (which, in many cases, we have had to keep anonymous) from our study.

STAGE 1: PRESSURE FOR BREAKUP

Breakups do not happen because the CEO sits in his hot tub and cries "eureka," or because the chairman reads a book on a plane journey commending breakup. In the future we hope they will. But in all thirty of our landmark cases, the breakup was preceded by outside pressure that meant that the corporation had approached, or was approaching, some crisis. The outside pressure was usually deep-rooted; it had been building for more than a year, and in some cases for more than a decade, before breakup was contemplated.

The pressure takes many forms. Sometimes it flows from stock-market underperformance (the share price lags that of similar firms); sometimes from the conviction of insiders and investors that the stock is undervalued compared to the company's assets. Sometimes outsiders and commentators suspect that the company's strategy has failed or is inadequate. Sometimes managers hear the heavy footfalls of predators, or see the shadows of suspected stalkers. Sometimes the pressure comes from powerful customers who are also the corporation's competitors. Sometimes bankers or preference shareholders apply the squeeze, arguing that debt is too high and pressing for an injection of equity. Sometimes the company experiences a need to raise extra cash, but finds no willing provider. Sometimes pressure comes from an industry regulator, pushing for the end of monopoly power and for greater competition. Sometimes there is a risk that part of the business could bring down the whole corporation, so that a quarantine is necessary for future security. And, very often, there is public criticism of the company's officers and their performance.

Sears felt the latter kind of pressure. At the company's shareholder meeting in 1992, five separate antimanagement proposals were tabled, supported by up to 41 percent of the votes. Major institutions demanded board representation, and that heads should roll. In the event the motions were defeated, but management clearly understood that the heat was on.

Even successful companies can come under outside pressure. Look at health care company Baxter International, in 1992 a very successful provider of medical devices and supplies to hospitals throughout the world. Baxter had built up Caremark, a profitable home health care business. John Gaither, vice president of corporate development at Baxter International, told us:

> The original arrangement was that we were in partnership with hospitals; but, after five years, some of our hospital deals ended because the hospitals didn't want to continue on a partnership basis, so we went ahead alone. This presented a problem: our home health care services were competitive with those offered in the same communities by our hospital customers. This provided us with an inherent conflict; the only thing we could do was to split the businesses up.

"Like many upheavals, the ICI demerger was driven as much by short-term pressures as by long-term managerial logic," according to Trevor Harrison, the company's former general manager of planning, in a comment in the *Harvard Business Review*. In May 1992, Hanson, the predatory conglomerate, took a 2.8 percent stake in ICI. Harrison confirmed that

> ICI regarded the move as a precursor to a hostile takeover, and a war of words ensued. By October, it was clear that Hanson would not launch a bid, but the episode underlined for ICI directors the urgent need to raise shareholder value. Investors would not tolerate indefinitely a situation in which pharmaceuticals supported low-margin businesses. Moreover, ICI would almost certainly need to raise new equity.

We saw in Chapter 2 that the most popular "official" justification for breakup was the desire for greater management focus on more limited markets and objectives. We approve of focus, and the desire for greater focus is usually genuine. But the corporations we studied did not decide to break up because they loved focus. They decided to break up because they were under pressure from the outside and because, eventually, reluctantly, and usually in a sideways manner, they brought themselves to see that breakup was the least unpalatable option available.

Lord Sheppard, former chairman of Grand Metropolitan, the liquor, food, and retailing concern, famously reflected on a chronically depressed share price: "If I'm not careful, some nineteen-year-old will come along and break me up."

Breakups do not arrive out of a clear blue sky. They come when the weather has already been unsettled for some time. And they usually come heavily trailed, after breakup has been mooted by outsiders as a potential solution to the corporation's difficulties. In many of our thirty landmark cases, there had already been discussion in the media or the investment community about the possibility, and usually the desirability, of some major corporate shake-up such as a divestment, a takeover of the firm, a new strategy or new management, or some other major structural change.

For Baxter, an article in *Crane's Business Daily,* a Chicago business newspaper, had strongly advocated the split years before it occurred. ICI had been dogged by recommendations in the business press and by stockbrokers that shareholders would be better off owning the pharmaceutical business as a separate entity. Similarly, Sears was beset by angry shareholders at an annual meeting.

For ITT, it was the stock-market rating that put breakup on the agenda. As Travis Engen, chairman, president, and CEO of spin-off ITT Industries, told us:

> The capital markets' influence was very important. In recent years capital structures and valuation approaches for different businesses have become more distinct. We found our capital market competitors could offer higher prices for

acquisitions because of their lower cost of capital. The difficulties this presented to the combined ITT were made clear in a 1994 meeting with the debt rating agencies. They were going to downgrade Hartford [the ITT insurance company] because the parent ITT was increasing leverage to acquire noninsurance businesses. We began to realize that we could not capture the opportunities and growth ITT wanted without jeopardizing Hartford.

So, the first thing is that the heat is on.

STAGE 2: RESISTANCE AND ACQUIESCENCE

"We didn't want to break up our corporation," an insider confided to us. "We had a successful history as an independent company stretching back to the 1930s. We felt we were established and, if you took a long enough time period, highly successful. There was a lot of emotional attachment to the old company. We were proud to work for it. Even to consider breaking it up seemed like sacrilege. How could we do this to the firm to which we owed our loyalty?"

Whenever we have been able to obtain the inside story of a breakup, interviewees have told a similar story. Breakup did not burst onto the agenda as an exciting, positive new possibility, like taking over another company. The idea of breakup arrived, more typically, like an unwelcome guest from a foreign land.

"I must admit that I initially opposed the idea [of breakup]," Travis Engen of ITT acknowledged to us. "To me it was an admission of failure—that we were unable to find management approaches which took advantage of the breadth of the company. But I came to believe that in remaining a single company we would find capital market forces preventing us from the kind of growth that would be available to us as separate companies."

In our experience, the very idea of breakup always engenders significant internal opposition. At ICI, the chairman, Sir Denys Henderson, reluctantly concluded that demerger was necessary to preserve ICI's independence in the medium term. Yet it was necessary to conduct an enormous amount of internal discussion, and to introduce a trusted outsider from ICI's merchant bank to be a catalyst for change and wear down the internal opposition.

Sir Denys was wily and wise. Soon afterwards, Michael Miles, the CEO of Philip Morris, was toppled after he advocated splitting the company's food operations from its tobacco side. Not surprisingly, Geoffrey Bible, Miles' successor, claims that there is "tremendous and powerful synergy" between food and tobacco: "Our management and board were convinced (and remain convinced) that splitting the company would have diminished, not increased, shareholder value over the long term." (Al Ries, *Focus*, HarperCollins, New York, 1996)

Gradually the board decides to pursue a breakup, but with reservations. We have uncovered not one single case where the decision was taken in a gung-ho spirit, where the decision-makers were raring to go and get on with it. Typically, it is acquiescence long before enthusiasm.

At one company, the acquiescence was a long time coming:

The idea of breaking up had bumped along as an idea for several years. Gradually I became convinced that we could not ignore the capital markets. . . . Breakup was considered confidentially by the top three or four people including myself and the chairman. In June of 1995 we finally presented a formal board paper and it was agreed—but not without opposition. It was a tough call.

This entire process of fighting the outside pressure and its implications is understandable. Businessmen live in a constantly challenging and threatening world. Their days are spent responding to competitive onslaughts, government inquiries and investigations, staff resignations, and so forth. Initially the pressures that lead to breakup can be seen as just one more problem to be dealt with and gotten rid of before moving on to the next one. Eventually, however, the problem is recognized as one that won't go away. That is when acquiescence begins and breakup planning gets onto the agenda.

STAGE 3: BREAKING UP

The third stage, the execution of the breakup, typically takes between ten and twelve months. It falls into two parts: the financial and technical side on the one hand, and the managerial on the other.

The financial arrangements and associated legal and tax considerations involve commissioning and coordinating a small army of advisers: investment bankers, brokers, lawyers, accountants, tax advisers, marketing experts, corporate identity gurus, and all manner of other specialists. Our interviewees report that the advisers are always expensive but usually competent. But some roadblocks proved troublesome.

Dividing corporate debt between the new entities can be difficult. Travis Engen of ITT:

> The major hurdle in separating was how to apportion the debt. As a balanced diverse corporation, we could carry higher levels of debt for the same debt rating. As separate companies, we would not receive this "conglomerate premium" and would be forced to place too much debt on the separate businesses. That's why we sold off the financial business . . . the proceeds were used to reduce the debt to be apportioned . . . this was a penalty to breaking up.

Charles Schalliol, head of corporate finance and investment banking at Eli Lilly, highlighted some other anxieties:

> It [the breakup] took a lot of time and was complex. As a consequence, there were some sleepless nights because there was always the risk of market failure. While we were going through this process the market could have fallen apart and we might have had difficulty marketing our new securities.
>
> We managed the process with a small team but it was a very big job; it was massive and complex. We anticipated this and allowed a target of completing the whole thing in eight months. It took us ten.

The managerial issues are even more complex than the financial ones. A number of important details must be settled. The lines of demarcation between the new entities must be carefully drawn and communicated, so that no one is in any doubt about his or her new home. Managers who have experience in more than one company must know where they are to fit in the future. Ongoing links between the new companies, if any, must be considered and negotiated. Quite often, the business units previously drew on a common pool of central or technical resources; these must be redeployed, set up as independent profit centers, or disbanded. The role of head office and its regional or divisional offshoots must be reviewed. These reviews cannot be carried out without some pain.

"Inevitably, the separation of two sets of businesses that had been united for more than 50 years involved some transitional pain," observes Trevor Harrison of ICI's breakup.

Recurrent themes are the pain of breaking up and need for speed to get the process over. Assistant Treasurer James Flaws of Corning elaborates:

> The process of going through the spin-off has been very painful. We have had to involve the operating managers in the process because it would have been impossible to plan the spin-off without them. We need them because they know the laboratory business well and will be running it after the spin-off. However, the change from our major strategic push to grow this business with a series of acquisitions had left the management with the impression that we are giving up on them, which is demoralizing. The result has been hurt feelings, distraction, and weaker results.
>
> My advice is that the faster that you can complete the spin-off the better off the business will be. While the process is going on, there is bound to be erosion in the business.

While agreeing on the need for speed, Sir Colin Southgate, head of Thorn EMI, noted that the corporate staff masterminded the breakup process, without seriously bothering the operating companies:

> If I were doing it over I would have moved faster to clear the decks. . . . The best thing we did in this whole project was to manage the project ourselves. We couldn't have done this eleven months of work any faster. . . .
>
> The project was really an exhausting and incredibly complicated proposi-

tion. We had holding companies around the world and had to get permissions everywhere. The whole structure of what we did was driven by US tax considerations. They [the IRS] are by far the most difficult authorities to deal with anyway.

Running the project in-house really worked well. We had a partner from our law firm seconded here and he basically managed it. Thus we did not have a second security house and their lawyers second guessing everything we did. The only outsider was this lawyer and he was tremendous.

In a deal such as this, the banks have their own axes to grind. And all of these long form reports that we had to go through. Why did we need this? We were just splitting up the business and giving it to the same people. Nobody was being disadvantaged . . . Even the way we split up the debt was basically down the middle. . . . It's the paperwork that kills you. . . . We figure that we generated seventy tons of paper. It could not all have been necessary. . . .

Another thing that was tough was the milk round of institutional presentations after the announcement. It was three weeks of slog. Our people got tired . . . But we managed and held it very tight. I can't imagine what it was like at ICI; I hear they had seventy lawyers working on the deal. . . .

While all this is going on, it is important to keep the business moving. The way we organized it [within the head office], it was not a big problem, since operating management wasn't much involved. Of course the top people were, but for the most part the people running the individual businesses only had to be consulted from time to time and were left to actually run them.

Travis Engen of ITT held, against the balance of opinion, that the breakup process was fairly straightforward and smooth:

It all went very well. It was amazing. We were helped by the fact that we have always had a business philosophy of facing our customers, not a focus on internal trading arrangements. . . . The internal linkages were not significant. . . . On the other hand, we had some 500 legal entities. This, of course, reflected a number of factors, particularly tax efficiency. It took a couple of years to wind all of that up.

Particular concerns arise. Several of the breakup participants we interviewed mentioned worry about the debt being attributed to spin-offs. David Clarke, chairman and CEO of US Industries, spun off by Hanson in 1994, recalls the concern of employees:

> The biggest anxiety was not with me and John [president, John Rao], but with a substantial number of our employees suddenly going with a debt-laden company. . . . The first six months were ones of anxiety; many people don't like change and they are concerned about their security. In our case, they asked the question, "How will they get our debt repaid; how will we survive?" People have to feel secure; these demergers all create this sort of worry. The key is to communicate and allay the anxieties.
>
> They have to know what the plan is, they have to know that there are a lot of strengths. It's the middle managers and the division people that have the greatest anxiety; the senior people are big boys and they can take care of themselves. In our case what we had to do was to rivet our attention on getting the debt down . . . that was the one thing which would build confidence for both our employees and our investors.

Many of our respondents stressed the importance of fostering cordial relations between the divorced partners. Baxter's John Gaither contrasts the mistakes made during the first Caremark spin-off with the far smoother 1996 parting with Allegiance, the distribution and health-cost-management operations:

> The spin-off of Caremark was an extremely painful process. Between the two businesses, Caremark and most of the rest of Baxter, a major customer–supplier relationship was not going to remain (unlike our current split-up). So, as soon as the spin-off was announced, everyone formed into their own camps; there was a tremendous level of hostility.
>
> This breakup is very different. There is no relationship about to be ended. The split allows both sides to align our cost structures, our culture and our investment strategy along business lines . . . so the commercial arrangements are clearer and more businesslike.

We have made tremendous efforts communicating what we are doing . . . we were guided by five agreed principles. My concern was that we had a framework beforehand to resolve problems as they arose. We went to an enormous amount of work with presentations, transition newsletters every two weeks and a lot of discussion and conversation. The whole idea was to keep the rumors manageable and to address problems as they arose. . . .

The company reaction to the breakup was one of surprise, but we are managing it. Now it's like two people getting divorced but remaining friends. It's difficult but it's working well.

Throughout the process, some anxieties will inevitably emerge. Concerns that were apparent include "loss of global clout" from becoming smaller in total revenues and political power, "lower purchasing power," "less choice of career path." What generally seems to happen is that these concerns are listened to, in some cases they are addressed, and in others they are virtually ignored. It seems to make no difference. Once the breakup has been announced, it cannot be aborted, and the concerns eventually evaporate.

STAGE 4: REBIRTH

The story has a happy ending. Phoenix-like, from the ashes of the old company, arise two or more vigorous new ones, each with its own style and distinctive identity. Despite the initial air of crisis, the reservations, the resentment of the outside pressure, the loyalty to the old order, the prevarication, doubt, and foreboding, it is hard to find more than a handful of managers who do not believe that the breakups were beneficial.

In both public and off-the-record conversations, assessments are overwhelmingly enthusiastic. "We're just much faster as a company than we were under IBM," comments Marvin Mann, CEO of Lexmark, a $2 billion printer and typewriter business bought by LBO specialists Clayton, Dubilier & Rice.

Like many breakup participants, Charles Schalliol of Eli Lilly believes that stock-price surges and tighter business focus vindicate the whole process:

It was all a remarkable success story. The breakup turbo-charged Lilly stock. A piece of distraction was removed. We are now virtually a pure pharmaceutical play. We have investor focus. Investors prefer to design their own portfolios and thus we are more attractive to them.

The Guidant spin-off has been a win-win proposition. It went public at 14½ and it is now 50. It has strategic focus and management incentives are aligned. Further, the management of Guidant have now had market discipline imposed upon them and that's got to be good for them. In the meantime, Lilly stock has more than doubled.

If there is one theme that keeps popping up as the major benefit of breakup, it is that of sharper focus. "What it's all about is management focus . . . most everything playing to their forehand," notes Steve Sanger, chairman and CEO of General Mills, of the spin-off of Darden Restaurants.

David Clarke, head of the Hanson spin-off, US Industries, agrees:

Because we have become a much smaller company (we went from $12 billion in sales to $3 billion in the US and then reduced the spin-off vehicle to $2 billion), we are really much more focused now, and we are running our own show. John Rao, president, said it best, "I can manage my own destiny."

This means that we can be more entrepreneurial, just like Hanson was in the old days . . . we are getting more performance out of the businesses; we are looking for higher growth.

Of course, some of the extravagant praise accorded to breakups by participants should be discounted as public relations hype or the effect of that psychological construct, cognitive dissonance: they would say that, wouldn't they? Yet, having looked into the eyes of dozens of breakup participants, and investigated the results, we are in no doubt that the enthusiasm is genuine, and most of the benefits claimed are real. Time and again, in managers who initially fight against the breakup concept, hostility gradually turns to skepticism, skepticism gives way to acquiescence, and acquiescence becomes first mild approval and then full-bodied enthusiasm. Indeed, there is often an evangelical ring to their conversion, which does not appear to wear off with time.

One of the newly converted declared that few large companies will be able to escape breakup in the long run:

> Looking back on it, I am very glad that I did it [breakup] even though I op-
> posed it at the outset . . . I guess we all have brighter futures. . . .
>
>   It seems to me that the whole process of breakups is inevitable. It is driven
> by the capital markets, but also by disclosure requirements. It is becoming dif-
> ficult to hide a laggard business because of increasing demands from share-
> holders and regulatory authorities to disclose every line of business.

The Sears saga is a premier case of revitalization of a moribund business through breakup. Chairman Arthur Martinez, the retailing executive brought in from Saks Fifth Avenue to turn around the retail operations, set the stage for his task: "Nobody in the company really understood who was shopping in the departments, who was making the purchase decisions. In almost every case, it was the woman in the family. And we didn't seem to care very much about her. The businesses we seemed to care about most were male-oriented: hardware, tools, automotive. There was a mistaken belief that these purchases were predominantly male-driven."

With a free hand and some capital to back him up, Martinez set about putting things right. Major staffing reduction and store closures ensued, the famed catalogue business was shut down, and merchandising strategies were clarified. As a result, Sears' retail operation is on the road to recovery. After a $2.9 billion loss in 1992, profits of $1.3 billion were posted in 1995, a 3.9 percent margin on sales of $33 billion.

Shareholders have profited from the breakup. Edward Brennan wrote in October 1995:

> If the Sears Merchandise Group had been a stand-alone business in 1990, ac-
> cording to company estimates, the price per share would have been $22. By
> June 1993, six months after Martinez had begun to restructure, the price would
> have been $27.12. Recently, Sears' straight-up retail shares were trading around
> $34. The 50 percent gain compares with a 45 percent plunge over the period
> in Standard & Poor's Composite Retail Stores Index.

In 1991, before breakup was on the agenda, the total market value of Sears was $8 billion. By 1996, the separate pieces were valued at around $36 billion.

Some questions remain. Sears' retail operations are focused and energetically run, but competing against Wal-Mart, Kmart, Discount King, and the category killers is, and always will be, tough. But now the story is different. Sears stands a far better chance of succeeding in this challenging competitive environment than it did in years past. Its balance sheet has been restored, and Sears is now run by a top management team that is clear about the company's direction. Perhaps more important, distractions have been eliminated. Homart Development was sold in 1995, and Prodigy, its on-line computer-service joint venture with IBM, went in 1996. Sears can now concentrate its considerable energies, virtually exclusively, on regaining its rightful position in the American retail pantheon.

Like those of Sears, executives who survive breakups come to love them, giving them wholehearted support, because they offer greater personal responsibility, because they relieve the business of bureaucratic head offices and other central encumbrances, because they make it easier to raise profits, and because they tend to give greater direction, purpose, and excitement to corporate life. In short, breakups work.

Tips for Successful Breakups

Our observations of the experiences of our landmark companies, together with our work with companies wrestling with the breakup decision and how best to implement it, have led us to some views on how to do it most effectively. We present them below in the form of a series of tips to guide the process.

Expect emotional resistance
Sell the positive aspects of breakup
Treat financial costs and outcomes as one input only
Create a breakup "credo"
Take positive managerial control of the project

Move as fast as you can

Communicate, communicate, communicate

Expect it to be a huge task.

1. EXPECT EMOTIONAL RESISTANCE

Breakup projects meet resistance. Not just from the self-interested, but also from serious, committed managers. Is this the right thing to do? Why are we doing it? Why can't we improve the way we manage, so that breakup isn't necessary? One manager we know captured it best when he said "My colleagues on the board looked at me with amazement and disbelief, like I was betraying the whole team." Breaking up is emotionally hard to do.

Our advice is more about being prepared than being armed. We have not found easy solutions to the emotional attachments managers have. Be firm. Sell the benefits of breakup. Where it is possible, give managers some time to get used to the idea. Experts on change say that emotional change has four stages: disbelief, anger, acceptance, and enthusiasm. Those who are resisting need time to get to the acceptance stage.

Picking the right moment is also important. It is hard to get senior managers excited about breakup when all is going well. Outside pressure can, therefore, be a useful way of ensuring that the issue rises to the top of the agenda. Breakup valuations are another way. If a company is clearly worth more in separate pieces, emotional resistance can often be breached.

2. SELL THE POSITIVE ASPECTS OF BREAKUP

While, on the one hand, breakup can be viewed as a traumatic assault on a way of life, the truth is that it offers a promising new lease on life to today's big companies. The irony is that it is less traumatic than many other forms of restructuring since the emerging businesses remain largely intact, with the freedom and incentive to decide on their own changes.

The alternatives to breakup—rationalizing the portfolio, downsizing the corporate center, restructuring divisions—are more evolutionary, but less attractive. These ways of reducing value destruction work to some degree, but they don't eliminate the problem. They are seen to be defensive moves. They sap morale and motivation. They leave the organization without a compelling rationale for its existence. Breakup needs to be presented to the organization as a positive step that will create renewed enthusiasm, fresh thinking, and allow two, three, or four companies to grow out of the original one. If breakup is seen as a defensive move, it is hard to win managerial support for it.

3. TREAT FINANCIAL COSTS AND OUTCOMES AS ONE INPUT ONLY

We have seen several companies consider and reject breakup because of the costs involved, or because the "exit P/Es" looked unattractive. The point here is that the main payoff from breakup is the end of value destruction. This can have a dramatic effect on performance, sufficient to dwarf the costs involved.

It is difficult to estimate the performance improvements that result from breakup. But it is essential to do so, since it represents the principal payoff from the exercise. Take heart from the major performance increases that consistently occur in spun-off companies.

4. CREATE A BREAKUP "CREDO"

Managing one of these exercises is not a wholly analytical, by the numbers, exercise. Frequent value judgments must be made and decisions with moral and emotional consequences must be dealt with. The making of these decisions behind closed doors can be a source of untold anxiety for those most affected.

Communicating intentions to all involved can help to allay anxieties. It can also facilitate decision making. This involves creating a framework, or a credo, for decision making that everyone knows and understands. It might address the importance of looking after customers during the whole process, expectations about staffing reductions and whether there will be any involuntary redundancies, and the way in which the two separated companies will interact after completion.

We have noted that a number of companies (e.g., AT&T and Baxter International) have attributed much of the success of their projects to the prior formulation of a constitution, credo, or statement of principles to guide the project, and for use as a reference point for the tough calls.

5. TAKE POSITIVE MANAGERIAL CONTROL OF THE PROJECT

The temptation in a financially complex exercise of this nature is to leave the organization of the many steps and phases to your bankers and advisers. Our experience is that this is a recipe for higher fees, point scoring between advisers, and a more protracted schedule. A capable project manager who can orchestrate the various parties involved and ensure decisions are made is essential. If a suitable internal candidate is not available, look for one in the financial or legal adviser and ensure he or she works on the project full time.

6. MOVE AS FAST AS YOU CAN

Once the decision to break up has been made and the managerial structure is in place, there is a strong rationale for getting through the whole process as quickly as possible. Inevitably, the longer it takes, the more expensive it becomes. Managing anxieties among the central staff and the rest of the work force grows in difficulty with each passing month unless exceptionally well handled. And the distraction brought by a project of this nature can damage the business.

Speed also brings with it positive benefits. As one strategic planning manager explained:

We decided to split the planning function early on. In part as a symbol and in part as an experience. We wanted to know what it was like, and it was quite an eye-opener. Although we still had offices on the same floor, we now had no reason to coordinate. We began to draw apart, and we began to feel the benefits: less time on coordination, more focus, more freedom, more energy.

A final benefit of speed relates to stock-market volatility. Once the process of breakup has been started, it is nearly impossible to stop. A faster process reduces the chances of a market collapse that could undermine the financial logic of breakup.

7. COMMUNICATE, COMMUNICATE, COMMUNICATE

We have been constantly reminded and impressed with the need to keep talking to affected employees during the course of the project, to keep them informed, and to find ways to allay anxiety as much as possible. When the center goes silent, when nothing is heard, rumors begin to circulate, undermining confidence and sapping energy.

Since the bulk of the work is generally performed by a few people at the corporate center and the divisions, there is a temptation to get on with the job and explain later. It's better to launch a special breakup newsletter that documents progress and setbacks than to let the cynics or the anxious spread half-truths and fears.

8. EXPECT IT TO BE A HUGE TASK

Our parting shot on this subject is that the whole process from beginning to end is likely to be protracted, demanding of a lot of management time, expensive, at times traumatic, and occasionally nerve racking.

Every person we have spoken to was surprised at how much work is involved for what seems, conceptually at least, like a straightforward task. Be prepared. Sir Colin Southgate, chairman of Thorn EMI, had been preparing his company for breakup for nearly ten years. Even so, the process still took almost a year and "it was an exhausting and incredibly complicated proposition."

Breaking up *is* hard to do. But, for many companies it is necessary. The alternative of fighting a rearguard action against a creeping tide of value destruction is much harder. None of those who have been through the process regrets it or believes the effort was wasted. They would all do it again.

Chapter 6

Profiting from Breakup

It is impossible to make such a radical change in our economic system
without creating losses as well as gains. To become a winner in the
breakup process requires the right investment strategy.

Investors should avoid breakups where there is no release of value
destruction.

As we have explained, we expect one of the beneficiaries of breakups to
be investors, who can expect to see increases of 20 percent or more in
the value of their shares. But there will also be losers. As always, some investors will misjudge events, selling the shares of overdiversified Multibusiness Companies (MBCs) too soon or too late, missing the importance of the
shift toward Focused Business Companies (FBCs) and single businesses. It is
impossible to make so radical a change in our economic system without creating losses as well as gains.

Chapter 6 therefore suggests investment strategies that will help individuals put themselves among the winners rather than the losers. There are four
generic investment strategies that may help to take advantage of the breakup
money machine:

Speculate ahead of a breakup
Avoid breakup candidates
Invest in a broad portfolio of breakups
Invest selectively in particular breakups

1. SPECULATE AHEAD OF A BREAKUP

If a breakup stops value destruction and leads to value release, a logical strategy is to work out which companies may break up and invest in them before other investors have driven the price up and before an official breakup announcement is made. Indeed, it seems to be true that US companies that have undertaken breakups generally experience two bumps in their share prices: first when there is initial speculation about a possible breakup (sometimes caused by a surprise announcement that the company is examining its options) and second when the breakup is announced. Investments under this strategy can either be liquidated for a quick profit or held to realize the likely subsequent appreciation.

But this strategy is easier to apply in theory than in fact. There are four objections to it:

1. You have to know ahead of the market which companies are likely to announce breakups. It is relatively easy to establish in principle which companies should undertake breakups, and even to create a league table of suspected gains from breakups relative to market value. The Breakup 100 can help you do this. You can even do it intuitively based on two simple principles and still not be far out: First, value destruction is likely to be greatest where one division appears to be held back by the center from taking the action it should. Second, value destruction is also likely to be greatest where the company is highly complex and the division's businesses appear to have different rules for success.

It is not difficult to decide which companies should be broken up, but it may still take years for the companys' leaders to come to this conclusion. Our research indicates (although this may be changing) that most breakups occur because external pressure to do something major becomes irresistible and because breakup is the least unpalatable of the viable options. It is difficult for outsiders to know when the company is about to bow to pressure. The existence of the pressure is not in itself a predictor; it can even be counterproductive in the short term if it hardens management's resistance. Knowing when the company has run out of road, or when a board is about to change its mind, must always remain either inside information or speculation, neither of which underpins a sound investment strategy.

2. The process is uncertain and can take a long time. The breakup may never happen, or may happen a long time after you have invested. Many breakup candidates are the subject of breakup rumors for years before the breakup; many have been perennially rumored to be breaking up and have not yet succumbed.

3. The gains may be small relative to the holding period. Typically, the two bumps in price (when speculation begins and when the announcement is made) are around 3 to 7 percent. This compares unfavorably with much larger surges in price on the announcement that a company is to be taken over.

4. Since there is a large number of potential breakup candidates, this cannot be a complete investment strategy: you need also to look at the commercial prospects of your target as well as the breakup probability.

It is dangerous to ignore investment fundamentals. There are so many candidates deserving breakup that are generally bunched quite closely in terms of merit, and the certainty that anything will happen quickly is so elusive, that the sensible investor starts to look at the intrinsic merits of the possible investments: is each company undervalued, overvalued, or fairly valued on the fundamentals? Yet once you start to introduce such considerations, the simplicity and purity of the investment strategy are violated and it becomes much less attractive.

On balance, we think this strategy does not have much going for it. It is speculation rather than investment. Only if the premium on announcement becomes much greater—and we will argue that this should be the case—would this strategy become either desirable or necessary.

2. AVOID BREAKUP CANDIDATES

In contrast to the previous strategy, it can be argued that a good strategy is to avoid investing in breakup candidates altogether. Instead, invest in companies that have a low value on the Breakup 100, because they are more likely to be better focused.

We have argued that single businesses and FBCs will outperform because they produce less value destruction. Since it is hard to predict when an over-diversified MBC is going to break up, it may be better to avoid MBCs altogether.

The investor can make his or her own judgments about which companies are single businesses and FBCs or use the Breakup 100 as a guide. If the logic is sound, a portfolio of single businesses and FBCs should outperform a portfolio of MBCs that do not break up.

One caveat is important. Single businesses and FBCs are liable to diversify. Dissatisfied with a tightly focused business, management often goes in search of excitement, growth, new adventures, and greater stability in other businesses. This is how old-style MBCs are created. Not only are these diversification strategies value destroying in their own right (the new businesses are acquired at a premium), but the MBC that is created destroys even more value in the ways we have described. Single businesses and FBCs that become old-style MBCs are likely to be the worst performers of all. Any investment strategy focused on single businesses and FBCs must, therefore, contain a rigorous process of weeding out any management teams that start to diversify.

3. INVEST IN A BROAD PORTFOLIO OF BREAKUPS

A further strategy is to invest after a breakup has been announced. In theory breakups will release suppressed value, especially for spin-offs that become single businesses (likely to be the smaller spin-offs). And the data say that the theory is correct. Breakups do release great value, especially in the case of smaller spin-offs.

The strategy to avoid risk is to invest in all breakups immediately after they are announced. Thus a kind of tracker fund can be constructed for breakups. We expect that enterprising fund managers will soon launch such funds. Consequently, we expect the premium on announcement of a breakup to rise. However, we hope that it does not rise too far, too fast, because that would undermine this strategy.

An additional twist on this strategy would be to invest in all breakups immediately after they are announced, but subsequently sell any pieces of a breakup that remain MBCs. Using our logic we would expect the single business and FBC pieces to perform better after the breakup than the MBC pieces. The world has changed much more radically for the single businesses and FBCs that are broken off. The MBCs that are broken off, or remain as the rump of the original, will have changed much less. They are now smaller and may as a result have fewer opportunities to create value from, for example, lower borrowing costs. They still, however, have the same forces for value destruction. By selling the MBCs and holding the single businesses and FBCs, the investor should do substantially better.

This strategy is also conservative but administratively more difficult. It requires a constant flow of business news and the ability to move quickly on receipt of the appropriate information. It is one for professionals or obsessive amateurs.

4. SELECTIVELY INVEST IN PARTICULAR BREAKUPS

For investors who are prepared to do more homework and to take more risk, a fourth strategy is to work out where the benefit from announced breakups is greatest, and invest only in those breakups that are likely to increase in value most.

Remember that the benefit of a breakup is the elimination of value destruction. Where value destruction is high, the benefit of the breakup is large, and its performance should improve dramatically. However, the best investment strategy is to find breakups where there is likely to be an additional increase in share price—from a subsequent acquisition.

Breakups are apt to be acquired when they are single businesses or small
FBCs that fit well with the portfolio of another company. In fact the acquisition price will be highest when the breakup fits with the portfolios of four or
five cash-rich and acquisitive companies, because they will bid the price up.
In the current market, any single business or small FBC (or even large FBC)
in the food industry with good brands and potential for international expansion will be attractive to Philip Morris, Nestlé, Unilever, and a host of small
players. These businesses should fetch high premiums.

Selective investment involves, therefore, identifying those breakups that
will benefit most from separation and will be attractive to acquisitive companies looking for extensions to their FBC portfolios.

With this approach, when to sell? The answer is: on acquisition by a third
party or after three years. US tax laws require potential acquirers to wait for
two years after a spin-off. It is thus in the third year that any acquisition activity is apt to take place. If the breakup does not become a takeover target,
it is difficult to know how long to wait to ensure that all the benefits of the
performance improvements have been realized. Experience with LBOs and
MBOs suggests that three years may not be a bad guess.

It should be noted, however, that there is not always a big price gain following the announcement. This is because there is already anticipation of
the gain before the announcement. Market rumors in some cases swirl
around breakup companies for years before the decision is formalized. Like
takeover rumors, once the change is anticipated and widely believed, the
share price reflects whatever the benefits are expected to be.

But sometimes there is a more fundamental problem in shareholder gain:
the market does not react at all. Whether or not there are rumors, whether
there is any anticipation of the likelihood of breakup, the share price stays
steady. Then the formal announcement occurs and still nothing happens.
Why might this be the case?

A lack of investor reaction can be for one or more of three basic reasons:

1. The market may simply not believe there is any significant degree of
   value destruction that will end on breakup.

2. The market may believe value destruction is rife, but that it will continue after breakup.

3. The breakup itself may cause new patterns of value destruction.

The first of these, where the market sees no value destruction to be terminated, can take place when the corporate center has been functioning largely as a holding company and doing nothing more to influence business decision making than to press for high levels of performance and stretching goals. But there is no large bureaucracy, no meddling by staff departments, no forced strategy changes, none of the worst value destroying kinds of behavior we have seen in other breakups. The investor contemplating such a breakup says to himself, "Wait a minute, how much improvement in the fortunes of the spun-off company can I really expect?"

Alternatively, and far more disappointing, is that the market may see the breakup as having no effect on value destruction. The new pieces of the company may continue to look and behave like the prebreakup MBC. The same people may be running the different pieces of the business and the same sorts of activities, processes, and behavior may stay in place. And perhaps even at a higher cost, as some central services—those which previously enjoyed a modicum of scale economy—are decreased in size.

Finally, the process of breaking up may be extremely costly, sufficient to cancel out much of the benefit. It can amount to a new wave of value destruction. Professional fees in a breakup can be large. Everyone we spoke to who has gone through a breakup comments on how arduous the task was and how complex and drawn out, in terms of the need for expensive professional advisers.

Similarly, the center may have been artful in its corporate design of tax structures, dividend routing, etc. The dissolution of the company usually means unwinding these structures with the prospect of paying more tax.

Obviously, the promise of a new dawn must have something behind it. Just breaking up does not release value. There must be an end to value destruction, assuming it was ever there in the first place. And it must be captured at an acceptable cost.

We believe that the very disappointing market reaction to the breakup of Hanson plc in Britain contained a bit of all of these problems. The old Hanson may have run out of attractive deal-doing material, but it was still very good at exacting superior performance from ordinary businesses. It did not interfere to any great degree in detailed management decision making. Indeed its very small central staff would simply not have had the time to do so. The market might well have judged there to be little value destruction to end.

Also, Hanson created two further MBCs—The Energy Group and Hanson Industries. Whatever concerns might have revolved about the old Hanson because it was highly diversified will not have ended because of the breakup. The diverse portfolio is still there in at least two of the surviving pieces.

Also, the transaction costs have clearly been huge—$150 million, by one estimate. And much of Hanson's intricate tax structuring is necessarily being unwound to enable the individual pieces to go their separate ways. Since the announcement, Hanson's share price has declined steadily.

A breakup is thus not a guaranteed free ride for investors. Usually it will be. But there will be those cases, like Hanson, where a release in value destruction does not happen. They are the ones for investors to avoid.

Breakup Strategies Outside the US

Should breakup work outside the US? The answer is plainly "yes."

It is difficult to read the evidence, because there is so much less of it. Only in the UK have there been enough breakups to even attempt a sensible answer. There have been 514 breakups in the US since 1980 and 389 since 1987. In the UK, since 1987 when the first breakup was recorded, there have been 43. This is clearly a much smaller and less reliable sample. There have, so far, been only a handful elsewhere.

For an investor, the safest approach is to invest in US breakups until it is proven that breakups elsewhere produce the same type of returns (as they should in theory). Only if the US strategy becomes unworkable (for example, if breakup stocks are bid up as soon as they become spin-offs, as the data suggest they should be) would it be better to invest in UK or other breakups.

Chapter 7

Breakup: The Future

Breakup is a gateway to better organization of large and medium-
sized corporations. It is the loudest, brashest, and most
exciting herald of a new order yet.

The prize is a trillion dollar opportunity, and the benefits of a
more effective capitalist system.

We hope by now that you are as excited as we are about the breakup movement. The sheer number and scale of the transactions that have been announced or have already been completed demonstrates the size of the prize. Most businessmen are pragmatic creatures. They don't vote for radical change unless the logic is overwhelming. From breakup, businessmen expect more energized organizations, a rejuvenated competitive position, and major financial benefits. They usually get it. And, after the breakup, there are no voices of regret.

But in order for all to benefit fully from breakup, we must understand the phenomenon. Much has been written about it that is misleading. Factors that cause management to take action are confused with the real source of the potential. We have explained the distinction. We have seen that the breakup movement is not primarily a financial engineering phenomenon, nor is it a fad. Rather, it is a gateway to a better way to organize our large and medium-sized corporations.

Where is all this leading? Are we seeing the end of big business? Is breakup the gateway to a new order? Or is it just another mechanism for tuning up the current order?

We believe breakup heralds a new order. It's not the first herald of this new order. Trumpets have been sounding for the past ten or fifteen years. Other heralds have been MBOs, LBOS, corporate raiders, unbundling, de-conglomeration, decluttering, and other ways of increasing focus. Breakup is, however, the loudest, brashest, and most exciting herald.

The new order is going to change the way most businessmen think. It is going to change the corporate landscape. There will be fewer diversified companies. There will be more single business companies. It will change behavior in the capital markets. It will bring into question the image of the generalist manager as hero.

In this final chapter, we look at some of the changes breakup is bringing with it.

THE EMERGENCE OF THE FBC

Multibusiness companies will only survive if they can demonstrate that they add more value than they subtract. Few pass this test today, and fewer will be able to do so in the future, as competitive pressures demand better and better performance. Some MBCs will survive, but they will be focused and exceptionally skilled at what they do. These newly focused MBCs will become FBCs—Focused Business Companies. Some, like Canon today, will be so much better in a number of related technologies than competitors that they will pursue skill-based competition in more than one line of business. Others, like Unilever, will be so much better at marketing fast-moving consumer goods than their rivals that they will be able to more than compensate for the disadvantages of being spread over several business areas (although we would not bet that even Unilever will be around in anything like its present shape in the year 2050, or perhaps even 2020). Others, like Emerson or

KKR, will exist because of the unique skills of the corporate center. They will focus on offering the business world their particular corporate medicine, acquiring businesses that need the medicine, and breaking them off when the medicine has worked its magic.

In the face of remorselessly increasing competition and specialization, FBCs are the only variable multibusiness configuration that can make sense in the longer term. Only FBCs can assemble the concentration of relevant skills to equip them to add real value to their businesses. Businesses are too diverse in their requirements for success for general management skills at the center to offer a useful service. Now the help from the center—the basis for corporate-level value added—must be focused, narrowly defined, and business-specific.

Some old-line MBCs will hang on, perhaps for decades. Some may preserve a role as industrial holding companies (rather like closed end funds or investment trusts), demonstrating such good judgment in buying and selling corporations that investors will tolerate their aberrant form. Berkshire Hathaway may be one of these. So long as Warren Buffett continues to create magic from his investment strategy, there will be no breakup. But on Buffett's retirement or when performance starts to slide, Berkshire Hathaway will likely be seen as just another expensive investment vehicle that takes out more value than it adds. (Of course, they could find another Buffett, but we wouldn't bet on it.)

General Electric (GE), led by the unique Jack Welch, is another gravity-defying MBC, prospering with its many lines of business and its extreme diversification. Frankly, we view both Jack Welch and Warren Buffett as magicians. Their successes are exceptions that prove the rule. GE is the six sigma event. Jack Welch has developed some corporate-center skills that appear to add value to a portfolio as diverse as GE's. Though many others have tried, Welch is one of the very few who has truly succeeded. With every phenomenon there are exceptions. Far from being harbingers of the future, they are odd events that make us gape in wonder. But they should reinforce our commitment to the future, not mislead us into thinking that the old-style MBC can survive.

The distinction between MBC and FBC is not always as evident as it might seem. Many MBCs are currently trying to squeeze themselves into the FBC's clothes. The logic most use is synergy. When ICI was under attack from Hanson, managers claimed fundamental synergies between the research activities of the company's chemical and pharmaceutical laboratories. Implicitly, they were trying to position ICI as a technology-based FBC such as Canon. Only two years later, management changed its sales pitch and argued that the technology synergies were negligible. ICI subsequently became Britain's largest breakup.

As we write, most companies are developing explanations for their diversity. They have to. Shareholders are on the warpath. They don't want to miss out on the windfalls to be had from breakup. What arguments are companies using? They are arguing focus. They are explaining their diversity by trying to hide it. A whole new art form is developing—the production of focus-sounding phrases that describe a company's portfolio: "leisure and related businesses," "chemical and specialty products," "electrical, electrotechnical, electronic, and associated products." These are all signs of MBCs trying to be FBCs. Don't be fooled.

Yet it is easy to be fooled. Only the detailed analysis of Chapter 4 can really separate the overdiversified MBC from the FBC. This is because the FBC is built around the skills and resources of the corporate center. If a corporate center says it has a special medicine that will work magic over its chosen portfolio of businesses, how are we to know whether we are being sold an MBC in the guise of an FBC? Moreover, shouldn't we give center managers the benefit of the doubt?

No. And this is a crucial message. In the future, corporate centers presiding over more than one line of business or one meaningful cluster should be guilty until proven innocent. If the story managers are telling is very convincing; if there is some track record, series of case studies, or business-level endorsement; if the businesses in the portfolio do not look like oil and water; then the guilty verdict can be held in abeyance pending a retrial. If, subsequently, the company does well compared to peers in the same industry, and the center continues to refine its corporate message, with more and more revealing anecdotes about how it is adding value and why its businesses are benefiting, then victory can be declared, and we can all rejoice in the birth of another FBC.

In other words, we should start with the assumption that all companies that are not clearly single businesses are old-style MBCs. We should only award them the FBC badge of honor once they have proved they are worthy of it. And we should watch them closely. Managers are prone to expansion. FBCs can quickly become diversified MBCs again. All additions to diversity should be challenged. Experiments should not be discouraged, but permanent increases in diversity should be put on trial in the same mood of skepticism. Until the MBC has been wholly discredited, it will creep back.

Even breakups can be MBCs masquerading as FBCs. Extremely diversified companies such as Hanson or ITT cannot bring about focus in our sense simply by dividing themselves into three or four corporate parts. Often there will be one "catch-all" receptacle to provide a home for the miscellaneous positions that cannot be clustered into a focused configuration. So ITT has its ITT Industries; Hanson, its Hanson Industries. At Hanson, another of the four breakups, The Energy Group, is also an MBC, scoring even higher on our analysis of the UK FTSE-100 than Hanson Industries. All such companies will eventually evolve, at a minimum, into FBCs. For many, the process will continue until only single businesses remain.

THE RESURGENCE OF SINGLE BUSINESSES

There will be a revival of single businesses. Single businesses will address one particular market area, and increasingly focus on one stage of the value-added chain (for instance, marketing rather than manufacturing, or distribution rather than retailing) and on one type of customer. Companies will narrow rather than broaden their scope. This is already happening. Consider the retail area. Department stores are having a hard time; specialists are replacing them. Specialists focus on one product category, like Toys 'R' Us, or on one type of customer within a product category, clothes for fat and tall people, clothes for the young and well off, even underwear for rich women.

The fastest growing car rental company now is not Hertz, but Enterprise Rent-A-Car, specializing in renting to people whose cars have been stolen or wrecked. In personal computers, the leadership mantle keeps passing from one specialist to another.

A single business will take care not to venture into so-called "related fields" or "adjacent segments." It will stick to its knitting. It will grow the product, or product/customer category. It will innovate, improve, and lower cost and price. It will expand geographically, and may ultimately become global, but it will stick to its single business. It will not want for growth. McDonald's has grown revenues and profits for decades, despite being confined to one narrow market; so has Home Depot.

Single business managers will believe that simple is beautiful. They will put their faith in economies of scale and in the virtues of pure market share, but will avoid the cost of complexity. They will carefully control their product lines, concentrating on the 20 to 30 percent of products that normally provide 70 to 80 percent of profits. They will outsource all functions where they do not have a competitive advantage. Single businesses will have the same simple organizational structures in all countries. They will constrain functional empires, despise overhead, and prefer the simple to the complicated solution.

While there will be a revival of the single business, there will still be some single businesses that move on to become FBCs. Wal-Mart, once a single business, is now trying to become an FBC, having moved into the wholesale distribution of grocery, music, books, and videos. Wal-Mart is using its retailing skills in these related areas. If it succeeds, it will become a retailing FBC. If not, it will be just another overdiversified MBC. Toys 'R' Us is also experimenting with its venture into Books 'R' Us. The difference in the future will be the cautious way that single businesses become FBCs.

In the past, single businesses have plunged into diversification whenever their core market turned down or they had spare cash. In the future, single businesses will tiptoe into new businesses, their senses on the alert for value destruction and their energies devoted to developing the corporate-center skills and knowledge that would justify the move from single business to FBC. Diversification will continue to be recognized as dangerous, or even worse. Entry into new businesses will require strong value creation logic or it won't be attempted.

THE ECLIPSE OF GENERAL MANAGEMENT

The US invented the idea of general management and has successfully exported it all over the globe, although the Germans and the Japanese have never fully taken to the idea. "Professional management," a body of knowledge acquired through a combination of industry experience and a spell at business school, became the route to riches for many after the Second World War. Professional managers hopped from firm to firm and from industry to industry on an ever-rising escalator of power and pay; the skills were believed transferable, so whether or not they should have been, in practice they were. Very often, "professional" managers brought a breadth of vision and commonality of view that resulted in industrial convergence; all industries tended to follow the same trend at the same time, from the rediscovery of marketing in the 1960s, to the trend to organic diversification in the 1970s, to the acquisition-driven feeding frenzy of the 1980s. Meanwhile, the US was losing international market share to German and Japanese companies, which had never believed in general management.

We now know that the idea of professional management, transferable across industries, is unproductive. From a management perspective, the differences between businesses are much more important than their similarities. Applying the lessons from hotels to restaurants is a recipe for disaster. The similarity is deceptive. Luxury hotels are quite different from budget hotels, city center hotels from those in small towns. Nor does expertise in accounting, discounted cash-flow analysis, information systems, or any other quantitative discipline equip an executive to make sensible decisions about baking, running an oil refinery, carpet retailing, or indeed about any other business.

FBCs and single businesses will not need "professional" managers in the current sense, nor will they give office space to generalists. The single business will need people steeped in its particular business, who love that business and cherish it. It will need outside advisers, functional or expert professionals who can provide skills the single business cannot build for itself. The FBC will need business specialists at the business level, and "focused" specialists at the corporate level. Even the FBC will need no generalists.

The message here sounds pretty radical. But it's not. It's common sense. We are not saying that business education (an MBA) is a bad thing. A good general education is a sound basis for most activities.

We are not saying that good accounting, discounted cash-flow analysis, and information systems do not help managers run businesses. We recognize that businesses often suffer from poor performance in these areas.

We are not saying that businesses can do without managers capable of integrating across functions—the business-level general manager. Individuals who can orchestrate manufacturing, marketing, IT, R&D, and other functions are the entrepreneurial life blood of any business.

What we are saying is that the general manager of a restaurant has completely different skills from the general manager of a software consulting firm, who has completely different skills from the general manager of a bus company. The differences between their skills are more important than their similarities, just as the differences between a tennis player, a football player, and a chess player are more important than their similarities.

The skills that are often referred to as "business acumen," "a good nose for business," "a safe pair of hands," "a good all round businessman" are not the important skills. What is important is the knowledge and experience of how to make a restaurant, a software firm, or a bus company truly successful. These are specialist skills.

At the center of an FBC, the skills are also specialist. They are skills that help the businesses improve. They may be about helping the businesses expand into China; they may be about helping the businesses transfer product knowledge across borders; they may be about helping the businesses squeeze out more efficiency or productivity. Whatever skills the FBC is built around, they are still specialist, not generalist, skills. And they are not easily transferred from one FBC to another.

General management skills, the skills that are at the heart of the profession of management, are important. They are about good administration; they are about problem solving and decision making; they are about people management. But they are only a small fraction of the reason for commercial success.

Sports provide a good analogy. Professional management skills are as important to business success as physical fitness is to sporting success. You could not imagine a business succeeding for long without good management, but good management alone is not enough. You need real talent at your chosen sport.

The general manager (someone who can lead any business) makes no sense to us in the same way the general sportsman makes no sense. The professional manager (someone who is capable of moving from function to function) also makes no more sense than the professional sportsman. To be successful in a competitive world you must specialize. Management skills, like fitness, are vital, but they only contribute a fraction of what it takes to win.

Once we have accepted that general management skills are a flawed ideal, many other attitudes will change. The thinking that causes management to diversify in order to spread risk—"we don't want all our eggs in one basket"—will die. Why would a manager want to have responsibility for something he or she does not fully understand? Why would an athlete want to compete in a sport he or she is not trained for?

Diversification will be shown to be a risk-increasing strategy, not a risk-spreading strategy. Similarly, the notion of "balance" will be equally exposed. Managers will not be striving to produce a balanced performance. They will be striving to excel. Managers will not be trying to smooth performance; they will be trying to maximize performance.

Attitudes to careers will also change. The underlying assumption of most career strategies today mirrors that of the old-style MBC. An ambitious manager expects to start life in a fast-track training program that gives exposure to a number of functions and businesses. In 1994, GE is reputed to have hired more than 900 graduates for its two-year training program. Each graduate joins one of a handful of functional homes and is then moved into four or so assignments in different environments over the next two years. What is this training the graduates for? To be a general manager, someone who will be able to run any GE business.

The sporting analogy is again instructive. We would not think it useful to give a promising tennis player exposure to football, the triple jump, and chess as part of his or her early training. Why do we think management or business is any different?

In truth, there are differences. In sports the rules don't change (at least not so frequently and unpredictably). Hence there are benefits in flexibility, in broad vision, and in having multiple skills. But the benefits are limited and do not justify the placing of general management skills on a pedestal.

In the future, ambitious businessmen will have a much more focused attitude to their careers. They may have what the British philosopher and guru, Charles Handy, calls chunky careers: they may specialize in one area or one business for ten years and then change direction dramatically, and specialize in another business or corporate-center skill for the next ten years. What they will stop doing is setting their sights on gaining entry into the top ranks of general managers as an end in itself.

A CHANGE IN THE CAPITAL MARKETS

The Anglo-Saxon capital markets, dominated by the activities of investment banks and stock-market quotations, may change dramatically as a result of the breakup trend. We do not know how far our capital markets have been shaped by the MBC, but we feel that the future will be different.

Big mergers and acquisitions will be confined largely to the building of global positions in industries where the acquirer possesses sustainable levels of competitive advantage. This will be particularly true in those industries like ethical drugs, which demand a global stance—access to all markets, and the ability to locate each stage of the value chain in the best possible place.

The merger and acquisition activities of investment banks will begin to wane. In the short term they will make a killing from breakup transactions. There will be merger and acquisition activity among small companies as single businesses form into FBCs, family-owned businesses change hands, and single businesses acquire competitors to build scale in their chosen product. There will also be a continual flow of breakups and deconglomerations, as failed FBCs retreat. What will reduce, however, are the megadeals, the hostile takeovers, the portfolio churning as one MBC rationalizes its portfolio, selling its businesses to other MBCs on a diversification drive.

In will come more long-term investment attitudes, as institutions choose the businesses in each sector they want to invest in and hold for the long term. Security analysts will begin to learn how to pick long-term winners, rather than simply assessing this year's earnings prospects. Long-term investment strategies will make more sense because businesses will be more stable.

In today's MBC dominated world, companies change strategies in search of size and growth, as a result of changes in sentiment about diversity, and in line with the scarcity of availability of money. In tomorrow's world, companies will be more stable. Single businesses will remain single businesses for generations. FBCs will develop and refine their corporate-center skills (their medicine), only changing when the flow of patients dries up or the medicine stops being effective.

This stability will give confidence to the long-term investor. Perhaps companies will no longer see the value in stock-market quotations. Institutions will be comfortable investing directly in companies, expecting to retain their holdings for decades.

Tomorrow's world, without the feeding frenzy of MBCs, or the fallacies of diversification, generalist managers, and size for size's sake, will be different.

Its effect on our capital markets will be profound. We can expect a move away from the stock-market-dominated roulette wheel version of capitalism to a more stable, more considered, more wealth-creating future.

BIG BUSINESS VERSUS SMALL BUSINESS

If big business is progressively broken up into many fragments, each a single business or focused cluster, does this mean that we will see an acceleration away from large firms and toward smaller ones?

Plainly, this is the short-term trend. But we should beware of too facile an answer. Focus does not necessarily mean small. Coca-Cola, after ending a foray into the entertainment business in the 1980s, is now focused. Its revenues are more than $18 billion, and its value on the stock market approaches $100 billion. Most people would not call Coca-Cola a small company. McDonald's has revenues of $10 billion and a market value of over $30 billion. McDonald's is a single business, but hardly small.

Counterintuitively, the reason that Coca-Cola and McDonald's are so large, especially in market value, may be *because* they are focused, not *despite* being focused. Coca-Cola is valued by the stock market at more than double PepsiCo. Coca-Cola and McDonald's have grown so big because they have focused on global expansion within a single business. They have been able to fund their growth because they are so profitable. They are so profitable because they focus on dominating their niches. Focus is the friend of sustainable growth, not its enemy.

So breakup yields another fundamental insight. It is not small that is beautiful, but simple. For any given level of complexity, it is better to be big than to be small. Simple, focused, profitable, and large is the best mix.

Therefore, do not expect the majority of breakups, these meteorites spun off by breakups, to remain in the shadow of their planetary parents. Of course they start much smaller than the megacorporations whence they came. But they also start with simplicity and focus on their sides. Many will eventually grow to become bigger than their parents.

Business has not run out of *lebensraum*, global space for expansion. Who knows which way the current balance between big and small business will tilt? But we would not want to bet on the small side.

AN ACT OF ENLIGHTENMENT, NOT SURRENDER

Breakup is a way of achieving greater simplicity. Breakup is a step back from the black hole of complexity. Where it is needed, breakup is an act of great managerial courage and wisdom.

This book has been written to persuade managers who see breakup as a last resort to change their minds: we want them to put breakup higher on their agendas. A decision to simplify, to encourage focus, to create two or three entities out of one, to eliminate value destroying behaviors, to provide more top jobs for leaders, to flatten management hierarchies, is no act of surrender. It is an act of true enlightenment.

"The Enlightenment" refers to a period in the eighteenth century when reason, scientific method, and humanitarians began to gain ascendancy over dogma, religious persecution, and feudalism. Stimulated by the science of Newton and the philosophies of Descarte and Locke, Europe and America moved out of the "dark ages."

Industrial capitalism is going through a similar "enlightenment." Stimulated by Michael Porter's concept of competitive advantage, the new "science" of economic value, and the recognition that government is not good at running businesses, we are moving out of capitalism's dark ages.

The market economy has triumphed over the planned economy; empowerment has triumphed over command and control; high-involvement management practices are triumphing over the traditional carrot and stick; and simplicity and focus are triumphing over generalism and elitism.

While there are some winners and losers in any major change, the age of enlightenment in capitalism, like the eighteenth-century age of Enlightenment before it, has many winners and few losers. The energy that is released more than compensates for the dislocations felt by the few. Because new capitalism is about throwing off constraints and value destroying structures, it is energizing in a way that benefits nearly everyone.

Corporate breakups are not just part of this new, enlightened way of thinking. Breakups will be seen as the great symbol of the new, enlightened capitalism: the symbol that corporate America and corporate Europe have thrown off the old ways for good. A symbol as important as privatization (or deregulation) has been crucial in confirming that governments have abandoned public ownership and embraced the market economy.

So don't shrink from breakup. Don't view breakup as failure. Don't treat it as a straw-man option, put up to scare the board into agreeing to an alternative. Think of the energy you can create by throwing off constraints and old mindsets. Put breakup high on the agenda.

Coda

An Appeal to Journalists, Analysts, and Management Writers

O ne of the problems we have encountered in promoting breakups is the degree to which managers are wedded to ways of thinking that reinforce the old-style MBC.

The most famous of these outdated ideas is the Boston Box or growth share matrix (see Figure 24). This analytical tool was designed in the mid-1970s to help managers of MBCs. During the 1960s, many companies had diversified, based on the view that professional management skills could be applied to any business. Harold Geneen's ITT was the best-known example. ITT became one of the world's largest conglomerates by using sophisticated financial control techniques. At least that is what people believed at the time. Many managers were influenced by the success of ITT and tried their hand at applying their planning and control techniques to a diverse range of businesses. With hindsight, we can now see that ITT's success was more due to the unique qualities of Harold Geneen than the sophistication of his control systems. His successor was not able to sustain ITT's enviable record of perennial earnings growth. Harold Geneen was a special phenomenon, not the forerunner of a better way to manage.

In the mid-1970s many of these diverse MBCs ran into cash flow prob-

FIGURE 24

The Boston Box

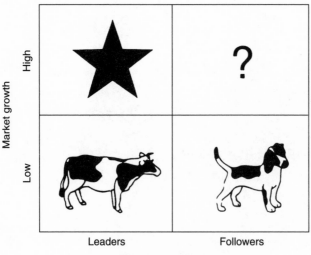

lems. They did not have enough cash to support all their businesses. The Boston Box was the solution. Corporate centers should place their businesses on the matrix and manage accordingly. Cash cows should be asked to deliver cash. Stars should be asked to deliver profitable growth. Dogs should be kept on a tight leash. Question marks should attract investment, if they had the potential to become stars. If the portfolio was not balanced—a good mix of cash cows, stars, and high-growth question marks—management should correct the situation through acquisitions and divestments.

It was a solution management felt very comfortable with. The language of cash cows and stars became woven into everyday conversation. Balance was seen to be a sound objective and diversification a good strategy for achieving it.

Yet the whole intellectual structure was built on sand. We now know that balance is not a sound managerial objective (shareholders can achieve balance much more easily and efficiently than managers), and that diversification is not a good strategy (it causes managers to take responsibility for businesses they don't understand). The Boston Box is analytically seductive. But the implications for management action have proved to be fallacious. Yet the concepts of "balance" and "diversification" have become deeply in-grained in the way many managers think. They have become almost sublim-inal, making it hard for managers to accept any ideas that do not fit with these principles. This is why we end with an appeal to journalists, analysts, and management writers. We need your help to correct this unfortunate sit-uation. It is not just about balance. Balance is the first of four fallacies that re-inforce the creation of old-style MBCs (see Figure 25).

The second fallacy is the belief that managers should be ensuring the long-term survival of the companies by investing in "attractive" business sec-tors. It is easier for shareholders to do this. The manager's role is to be skilled at maximizing the value of businesses, not doing something shareholders can do more easily for themselves.

FIGURE 25
Famous Fallacies

1.	*Balance.* Many companies diversify in order to spread risk and smooth earnings performance. Companies in cyclical businesses seek counter-cyclical activities; regulated companies expand into unregulated businesses; and companies dependent on one economy look for revenues in other currencies. The track record of these efforts has not been good. Companies that diversify to spread risk perform less well than mutual funds. Shareholders and fund managers, in countries with substantial equity markets, are better positioned to spread risk than business managers.
2.	*Attractive businesses.* Some managers diversify to invest in more attractive business sectors. These managers have low-growth or low-profit businesses and seek higher growth, higher margin businesses. Their performance has also been disappointing. The price they pay for attractive businesses is frequently higher than subsequent performance would justify. Because corporate managers must pay a premium for control, they are less well-placed than fund managers to move money into attractive sectors.
3.	*Growth and gap filling.* Many corporate managers diversify to fulfil a growth ambition. They use acquisitions to close the gap between expected earnings growth and a target, such as a growth of 15 percent per annum. This logic produces a performance as poor as those pursued by managers driven by a search for balance or attractive businesses. The premium paid for growth businesses rarely leaves any value for the acquiring shareholders.
4.	*Related businesses.* Managers have long been encouraged to limit their diversification to businesses that are related—in the same industry, selling to the same customers, or utilizing similar strengths. Surprisingly this synergy logic seems to fail almost as frequently as other logics. The reason is that synergy benefits are often more than offset by management's poor understanding of the new business.

A third fallacy is the belief that diversification is often necessary to meet growth targets. Managers in low-growth businesses argue that they cannot meet shareholder expectations unless they move into higher growth markets. The reality is that companies can only grow as fast as their skills allow. Moreover, growth is not a required condition. Most shareholders are interested in value creation, not growth.

The fourth fallacy is about synergy. Managers believe that they can release synergy by diversifying into businesses that are "related." This normally means that the businesses have common customers, suppliers, or technologies. In practice, related businesses often do not offer opportunities for synergy, or, if they do, the corporate managers do not discover how to release them. Moreover, diversifying into related businesses can draw managers into situations where they do not understand dimensions that are not related.

We believe that analysts and journalists have a big effect on management thinking. The senior managers we know pay attention to what is written: it affects their thinking. One chief executive who had previously been running a large (100,000 employees) government-owned business explained: "The very fact of having to talk through your strategy and get response through questions or brokers' circulars helps you understand how your business looks through the other end of the telescope."

The writings of journalists and analysts can, therefore, help to debunk these fallacies.

All too often, however, journalists and analysts reinforce managers' prejudices, by being too respectful of management's views, and by quoting what management says in a way that adds credibility to it. They ask questions that are rooted in fallacious thinking and fail to ask the questions that would expose weak thinking and help to debunk the fallacies.

KEY QUESTIONS

We do not want to tell other writers what to write, but we do want to ask for help in rooting out the poor thinking that is doing so much damage to our large companies. Our suggestion is that there are four questions analysts and journalists can ask that will help expose the problem.

1. Does this company consist of different kinds of businesses? In the language of Chapter 4, does this company have multiple "clusters"? Most do, and it is normally apparent from the company's annual report. If there is doubt, the question can be put to senior managers: "Do all your businesses have similar critical success factors or does your portfolio consist of different types of businesses?"

In the Appendix, the consulting firm OC&C used public information not only to define clusters but to judge how dissimilar they are. With access to management, it would clearly be possible to go much further in defining the clusters and assessing the differences. For companies with multiple clusters, the next three questions should be asked.

2. What kinds of help do the businesses in this company need from a corporate center? This question should be asked cluster by cluster. What sort of help do the businesses in cluster A need? What sort of help do the businesses in cluster B need? And so on.

It is a question that can be asked of central managers and business-level managers. The description of "improvement opportunities" and analyses suggested in Chapter 4 should help the questioner judge whether the answers he or she is getting make sense.

3. What is corporate management's reason for keeping the different clusters together in one portfolio? Watch out particularly for explanations that are rooted in one of the fallacies: "we are moving from tobacco into more attractive industries," "we believe that our commercial businesses provide a useful counterweight to our more volatile defense businesses," etc.

Watch out for weak reasons such as "we at the center can raise money more cheaply and provide a useful objective challenge to the business-level managers. We are a wiser banker than they could find as independent businesses." Ideally you would like the reason to be substantive, pointing to influence the center has that is likely to improve performance by 20 percent or more. Without a substantial amount of value added, most multicluster companies gradually succumb to the forces of value destruction.

Watch out, also, for cling-film descriptions, like "we are a leisure company," or arm waving on the subject of synergy, like "all our businesses are marketing oriented." Corporate managers have to produce public statements that explain the company to shareholders and employees. When these public statements use linguistic explanations for the portfolio, the underlying logic is usually weak.

4. What are corporate center managers particularly good at? This question is the most unsettling question that senior corporate managers can be asked. Yet it is the most relevant of questions. One of the most useful principles embedded in the managerial psyche is that of competitive advantage. Few managers reject the validity of the question "what are you better at than others?"

Yet this question is rarely asked of the corporate center and even more rarely of the chief executive. Analysts and journalists can ask it, with both innocence and respect. "What is it that you do here at the corporate center that makes you believe you can add value to the businesses you own? And, more importantly, what is it you do that makes you a better owner of these businesses than someone else?

Without advance notice of the question, most managers will give the sort of blustering answer we all give when we are asked what our strengths are. So give management notice of this question. Ask it more than once. Probe the answers. Ask for anecdotal examples. Ask for confirmation of these anecdotes from business-level managers. Don't let the fish off the hook. Forcing managers to face up to this critical question can be an important service to corporate managers, the company, and capitalism.

ENCOURAGING DEEPER THINKING

The four questions we are suggesting will help judge whether the company is an overdiversified MBC, a single business, or a value creating FBC. But this is not the reason we suggest them. We suggest them because we believe these questions will encourage management to think more deeply about their portfolios of businesses. The questions will also expose some of the fallacies we are concerned about, and they will provide some interesting answers for analysts and journalists to write about.

Once the value destruction that stalks the corridors of multibusiness companies is eliminated, economic performance will leap ahead. Breakup is, in our view, the best way of making this happen. But in the long run, we will keep value destruction to a minimum only if management thinking is embedded with a different set of principles. Managers need to replace the fallacies that have grown up around the diversified MBC with new principles such as "grow only as fast as your skills allow," "focused skills are likely to outperform generalist skills," "management structures breed value destructive behaviors," "own businesses only when you are the best owner," and "simple is beautiful."

This change in thinking will only come about if it is reinforced by commentators and writers. Analysts and journalists, in particular, have much more influence than most of them believe. If every corporate-level strategy was praised or ridiculed in the appropriate way, if every multicluster strategy was judged guilty until proven innocent, if every audience booed every time the word "balance" was used, we could make the transition to a new, more energetic, more value creating capitalism at twice the current speed. The torrent of breakups is leading the way, but managers will only change their root concepts if they understand why this torrent is occurring, why their root concepts are fallacious, and which new ideas to put in their place.

We hope this book will achieve some of these objectives, but we need journalists, analysts, and management writers of all kinds to carry the attack to chairmen, chief executives, directors, fund managers, shareholders, and investment institutions. The prize is the trillion dollar opportunity, and the benefits we will derive from a more effective capitalist system.

Appendix

The Breakup 100

To test our belief that many MBCs need to be broken up we wanted to develop a methodology for indicating, if possible, from public data, whether a company should be considering breakup or not. We wanted to confirm our view that many companies might be overdiversified.

We recognize that it is possible to recommend breakup only after a detailed internal analysis. Public data are not sufficient to provide answers to the important questions in Chapter 4. However, because our research had led us to speculate that more than half of today's MBCs should consider breakup, we wanted a numerical index to help us test this view and identify those companies that best fit our description of old-style MBCs.

We therefore sought the help of OC&C Strategy Consultants (a leading international firm of consultants) in undertaking a "top down" analysis driven purely by generally held market data. Despite having chosen what we consider to be a reasonable methodology, there is considerable room for debate about the individual companies. Such a debate misses the point. All companies should continuously strive to prove to themselves and investors their industrial logic. OC&C's task was to apply, albeit in a limited exercise, the methodology described below as objectively and consistently as possible and thus to give a logical, if not statistical/analytical, underpinning to our work.

THE BRIEF

We wanted OC&C to collect data that would help us make judgments about the forces of value creation and value destruction in large companies. We asked OC&C to help us to apply a consistent framework in assessing the following:

the potential for value destruction;

the rationale for believing there is substantial value creation;

the opinions of analysts who have an intimate knowledge of the company.

OC&C analyzed the companies of the FTSE 100 for the UK and the Fortune 100 for the US.

An initial pass was taken to determine which of these businesses were single businesses or MBCs. For the purpose of the analysis single businesses were treated as those with 90 percent or more of turnover from a single segment. For example, although American Home Products, Pfizer, Eli Lilly, and Merck all have businesses in both human pharmaceuticals and animal health, it is only for American Home Products and Pfizer that animal health accounts for more than 10 percent of turnover (actually 14 and 12 percent, respectively). Thus for the purposes of the analysis both Merck and Eli Lilly have been treated as single businesses.

In line with the methodology in Chapter 4, we believe that the potential for value destruction increases the more different the businesses are. If the businesses are similar in the types of customers, economics of the business, types of employees, etc., the multibusiness organization structure is unlikely to be much of a disadvantage. We therefore asked OC&C to consider the degree of difference between the critical success factors of the businesses in a company's portfolio. For example, the difference between car manufacturing and mortgage financing is high as is the difference between pharmaceuticals and toiletries. The difference between fixed and cellular telecoms, or tissue products and newsprint, is medium, as is the difference between pharmaceuticals and agrochemicals. A low difference would be between the soap business in the US and the soap business in Europe, or between hamburger restaurants and pizza restaurants.

Public data, however, do not provide organized information about the critical success factors of different businesses. OC&C, therefore, had to use surrogates. They decided to score companies on the degree of dissimilarity between their businesses, looking at:

management tasks
customers
technology
purchases
brand image
intertrading.

Clearly this is not a full list of all the factors you would want to take into account, but within the scope of the project we felt that this degree of dissimilarity would be a good surrogate for the potential of value destruction.

Companies with apparently large dissimilarities between businesses were awarded "high" ratings; those with apparently similar businesses were given a "low" rating.

The process for scoring the degree of dissimilarity is subjective. Only a limited amount of time could be spent on each company and a judgment was then made based on the information gained. To provide a check on these subjective judgments, OC&C also analyzed another possible measure of the degree of dissimilarity—differences in return on sales.

For example, a grocery retailing business has a return on sales of around 5 percent whereas a specialty chemical company will have a return on sales of around 20 percent. Differences in return on sales point to differences in the underlying economics of the business. The return on sales of an upmarket restaurant may be 20 percent, whereas the return on a mass market restaurant may be 10 percent. Return on sales (unless it is driven purely by performance differences) is, therefore, an indicator of dissimilarities. Its objectiveness makes it a useful test of the subjective judgments. By combining the scores we were able to produce a useful surrogate of the potential for value destruction.

Ideally, a judgment of value creation would be based on detailed knowledge of the impact the center's influence has on its businesses. Without this detailed knowledge we chose two surrogates: how convincingly management explains its portfolio in the latest annual report, and how well this company has performed versus its sector/peers.

From the annual report, we wanted to measure the degree to which each company had a sound logic for creating value from their portfolio of businesses. The logic could be about synergy between the businesses, for example, savings in purchasing costs, shared technical skills, shared knowledge of customers, and so on. The logic could also be about managerial expertise: the corporate center might have some special expertise in managing businesses in one sector, in one stage of the life cycle, or with a particular management task like internationalizing or rationalizing. If management provided a convincing explanation for the portfolio, they were given a "low" (propensity to consider breakup) rating. If there was no explanation, or if the explanation was unconvincing, they were given a "high" rating. Many fell in the middle "medium" rating category.

For example, 3M provides a convincing justification of its diversified product portfolio in two ways. First, it argues that there are a number of common technology platforms underlying apparently dissimilar products. Second, a culture of innovation and entrepreneurship fuels growth right across the business. This scored a "low" (propensity to consider breakup) rating.

On the other hand, American Home Products provides no explanation for the logic of operating in both pharmaceuticals and snack convenience foods. This scored a "high" rating.

Clearly the process of scoring what management said in the most recent annual report is both partial (there may have been a convincing explanation given in the previous annual report) and subjective. As before, therefore, this partial and subjective measure was paired with an objective measure—performance versus sector.

For each company, OC&C looked at the share price performance versus a suitable sector. Performance better than the sector is an indication that the company is doing something right. Performance worse than the sector indicates that the strategy is not working so well. The reasons for performance differences can be many, but it is a simple, objective way of testing how management's strategy is translating into market perception of value creation.

The final area of assessment is the opinions of analysts who have an intimate knowledge of the company. OC&C looked through analysts' reports on the company for indications that breakup should be on the company's agenda.

For example, some analysts recommend more focus:

> If management's initiatives are unsuccessful, and returns remain below the peer group averages and the cost of capital, significant portions of the business are likely to be candidates for divestment. We believe this would be a winning proposition for [Chevron] shareholders. (Morgan Stanley & Co., July 1, 1996)

In these cases companies were awarded a "high" score. Others raise the issue of breakup, then reject it:

> We do not want to evaluate IBM piece by piece (we believe breakup analysis is a silly argument for the stock). (Merrill Lynch Capital Markets, March 29, 1996)

In these cases, companies were awarded a "medium" score on the grounds that, although rejected by the analysts, breakup is on the agenda—the company should be performing this analysis on itself.

Others do not discuss issues of breakup or focus because, presumably, they are comfortable with the company as it is. In these cases, companies were awarded a "low" score. The opinions of these analysts are clearly important checks on the judgments OC&C made about the potential for value destruction and the logic for value creation. They were, therefore, given equal weight in the scoring system.

TESTS OF RELEVANCE

The scoring system we devised with OC&C was inevitably somewhat arbitrary. We gave equal weight to subjective and objective measures, and we gave equal weight to the potential for value destruction, our belief in value creation, and the opinions of analysts. To confirm that this scoring system was reasonable we ran three types of checks:

1. We changed some of the weights to see if this made a big change to the type of company that had high scores. We found that there were no obvious biases against any type of company.

2. We scored companies with which we were intimately familiar to see if the scoring system agreed with our "from-the-inside" judgment. Although there were differences, this test confirmed that the scoring system was reasonably effective.

3. We scored a sample of the landmark companies we had been researching. These are companies that had broken up or were in the process of breakup. Our scores for these companies confirmed that the Breakup 100 is reasonable. It also helped us calibrate the Breakup 100. We could reasonably assume that companies with scores higher than those of our landmark companies should, at a minimum, have breakup on the agenda.

Based on these three tests of the relevance of our Breakup 100 we gained sufficient confidence to publish the data. We also gained renewed confidence in our conclusion that over half of today's MBC's are overdiversified and need to consider breakup.

THE ANALYSIS

The following pages give the precise definitions used by OC&C, and they present a detailed analysis of the top 100 US companies as well as a sample of landmark companies.

This appendix does not give detailed analysis of the top 100 UK companies because of conflicts of interest. OC&C has a number of clients in the UK top 100, and would, therefore, not be in a position to publish judgmental data on these companies.

The detailed analysis of US companies gives some surprising results.

1. Some companies have a higher score than expected, for example, Johnson & Johnson and BankAmerica. By reputation, these companies are not known as being overdiversified. They are more likely to be held up as examples of FBCs.

In each case there is a reason in the scoring system. Both companies have had some elements of breakup discussed, and in some cases recommended by analysts. The analysts therefore believe it is worth considering whether there are significant parts of their portfolios that might be worth more as independent businesses or in sales to other parent companies. If the analysts' score was "low" rather than "high," or "medium," these companies would drop from near the top of the list to around the middle of the list. We gave brokers' views a double weight in the scoring system because they have detailed knowledge of the company often including conversations with management.

2. Some similar companies have rather different scores. Three industries illustrate the problem: pharmaceuticals, automotive, and oil. Yet the companies in these industries have widely differing scores.

> In pharmaceuticals the range is from rank No. 2 (American Home Products) to rank No. 76 (Eli Lilly).
> In automotive the range is from rank No. 4 (General Motors) to rank No. 76 (Chrysler).
> In oil the range is from rank No. 10 (Amoco) to rank No. 60 (Texaco).

The reason for these differences comes mainly from differences in diversification. In pharmaceuticals, American Home Products is involved not only in human pharmaceuticals and animal health, but also in packaged food products (a sector that brokers are arguing the company should exit); while Merck is more than 90 percent focused on human pharmaceuticals. In automotive, General Motors owns Hughes, a large defense, aerospace, and space electronics company (which it announced would be spun off at the time of this writing), while Chrysler has retrenched back to a business focused on automotive production (and financing).

Big differences can, however, also come about for other reasons. Amoco has the same "dissimilarities" and "brokers' scores" as Texaco, but provides no rationale for its portfolio and has a worse share price record.

The Breakup 100 is, therefore, not our judgment about what companies should do. It is not even our judgment about which companies should be actively considering breakup. (We would recommend that every MBC go through the analyses in Chapter 4 to check the validity of its current portfolio.) It is a consistent and coherent approximation of portfolio logic and thus its results provide a good view, relative to its peers, of the degree to which breakup should be on a company's corporate strategy agenda.

Using this rank ordering as our guide, we are comfortable concluding that more than half of today's large multibusiness companies would benefit from some form of breakup. At a minimum, they would benefit from breaking off a significant part of their portfolio. We arrive at this figure in three ways.

First, more than half of the MBCs have scores that are equal to or higher than those of companies that have broken up.

Second, our knowledge of individual companies in the bottom half of the list suggests that some of them should break up, implying that many of the companies above them would probably benefit from the same medicine.

Third, even companies low down on the list, such as the telecommunications giants, should not consider themselves immune from breakup. Pacific Telesis chose to separate its fixed from its cellular businesses, and, if this proves to give a better combination of value creation and value destruction, companies such as GTE, Bell South, and AT&T may want to follow suit. Current commentary suggests that the Pacific Telesis decision is not appropriate for other telecommunications companies, hence their low score. But, as this book is at pains to point out, current commentators do not fully understand the pervasive force of value destruction in MBCs. If Pacific Telesis can reduce value destruction and yet keep many synergies through arm's-length relationships, the net result will be in its favor and others would need to consider following suit.

BREAKUP 100: DETAILS OF METHODOLOGY

Sources

Data	Source
Details of portfolio	10K and/or annual report
Annual report rationale	10K and/or annual report
Segmental ROS data	10K and/or annual report
Share performance	Datastream
Brokers' reports	Context search of Investext database using "breakup," "spin-off," and "divestment" as search parameters

Overall Scoring

A numerical scoring system was used to arrive at the overall breakup score. Equal weight was given to each scoring category. A "high" score is 2; a "medium" 1; and a "low" 0.

Percentage breakup score was calculated by summing these individual category scores and dividing by the maximum possible score (adjusted for "not available" figures).

SBU Differences Scoring

Business unit difference categories were weighted as follows:

Category	Weighting
Management	2
Customers	3
Technology	3
Buying	2
Intertrading	1
Brand/Image	2

For example a company scoring a "high" in customer differences would receive 6 (weighting 3 × "high" score of 2) points in that category. All the weighted category scores are summed to give a total score, which is converted to a percentage of maximum. These percentage scores were split into quartiles and were converted to H, M, L format as follows:

Scores > 81 percent scored "high"
Scores of 51 to 81 percent scored "medium"
Scores < 51 percent scored "low"

ROS Differential Scoring

Return on sales differential was scored on the basis of absolute differences between the percentage ROS for the different business units as reported in the annual report. These were split into H, M, L format as follows:

Difference of >10 percent scored "high"
Difference of 5 to 10 percent scored "medium"
Difference of 0 to 5 percent scored "low"

Annual Report Rationale Scoring

This was scored as follows:

No rationale or unconvincing rationale scored "high"
Some rationale, though inadequate, scored "medium"
Convincing rationale scored "low"

Share Price Performance Scoring

Share price performance versus a relevant tracking sector was determined between 31 October 1991 and 31 October 1996. The data were split into quartiles and scored as follows:

Underperforming sector by more than 9 percent scored "high"
Performance versus sector from −9 percent to +40 percent scored "medium"
Outperforming sector by more than 40 percent scored "low"

Brokers' Reports Scoring

These were scored as follows:

A majority of brokers recommending a breakup scored "high"

A majority of brokers discussing a breakup, but not recommending, scored "medium"

No discussion of breakup scored "low"

Missing Data

In cases of missing data—for example, no segmental reporting for ROS differential—an "na" (not available) was entered. The company in question was then scored out of the remaining categories. For example, a company missing one category of information would be scored out of 8 points, instead of the full 10.

Breakup Rank	Size Rank	Company Name	Chosen Business Unit Comparison	Management	Customers	Technology/Manufacturing	Buying	Intertrading	Brand/Image	Overall SBU Differences Score
1	78	Viacom Inc.	networks and broadcasting vs publishing	M	H	H	H	H	H	H
2=	35	American Home Products Corp.	healthcare vs agricultural products vs food products	H	H	H	H	H	H	H
2=	83	Warner Lambert Co.	pharmaceuticals + consumer health care vs confectionery	H	H	M	H	H	H	H
4=	20	Bristol-Myers Squibb Co.	pharmaceuticals + medical devices vs health products + toiletries	H	M	H	H	H	H	H
4=	23	General Motors Corp.	automotive vs Hughes	H	H	H	H	H	H	H
4=	8	Johnson & Johnson	personal care vs pharmaceuticals + medical products	H	M	H	H	M	H	H
4=	13	PepsiCo Inc.	beverages + snack foods vs restaurants	H	M	H	L	H	H	H
8=	76	Banc One Corp.	retail banking vs commercial banking	M	L	H	L	M	H	M
8=	18	Berkshire Hathaway Inc.	insurance vs confectionery vs home products vs shoes	M	H	H	H	H	H	M
10=	28	Amoco Corp.	exploration & production + petroleum products vs chemicals	H	H	H	H	L	H	H
10=	38	BankAmerica Corp.	consumer + middle-market vs corporate	L	H	M	L	H	H	M
10=	25	Chevron Corp.	petroleum vs chemicals	M	H	H	H	H	H	M
10=	60	Emerson Electric Co.	commercial and industrial vs appliance and construction related	L	H	M	H	L	H	M
10=	4	Exxon Corp.	petroleum vs chemicals	H	H	H	M	H	H	H
10=	16	E.I. Du Pont de Nemours & Co.	chemicals vs petroleum vs fibers vs polymers	L	H	M	H	L	H	M
10=	27	Ford Motor Co.	automotive vs independent financial services (Associates & USL)	M	H	M	H	M	H	M
17=	85	Tele-Communications Inc.	cable and communications services vs electronic retailing and entertainment and information processing services	H	M	H	H	M	H	H
17=	95	Wells Fargo Co.	retail vs business banking	L	M	H	L	L	H	M
19=	69	Allied Signal	aerospace vs automotive vs materials	M	H	H	H	H	H	M
19=	59	ARCO	petroleum + coal vs chemicals and specialty products	H	H	M	H	L	H	H
19=	46	Dow Chemical Co.	chemicals vs plastics vs hydrocarbons	M	H	M	H	M	H	M

	No.	Company									Overall SBU
19=	93	First Chicago NBD	retail and middle-market banking vs corporate and institutional banking	M	H	H	L	H	H	M	M
19=	1	General Electric Co.	aircraft engines + power generation vs appliances vs broadcasting vs industrial products	H	H	H	H	H	H	H	H
19=	7	International Business Machines Corp.	hardware + software vs services	M	H	L	H	M	L	M	M
25=	44	American Express Co.	travel services vs financial advisory	H	H	H	H	H	H	M	M
25=	19	American International Group Inc.	general & life insurance vs financial services	H	L	H	H	H	L	H	H
25=	41	Eastman Kodak Co.	consumer imaging vs commercial imaging	H	L	L	H	H	L	M	M
25=	70	First Data Corp.	transaction processing vs healthcare claim processing	M	L	H	H	M	M	H	L
25=	47	Gillette Co.	personal grooming vs stationery products vs small electrical	M	M	H	L	H	M	H	M
25=	86	Heinz HJ Co.	food vs pet food	L	L	H	L	L	L	L	L
25=	73	Lockheed Martin Corp.	aerospace + electronics + space and strategic missiles vs IT Services	M	M	M	H	M	H	M	M
25=	17	Mobil Corp.	exploration & production + marketing & refining vs chemicals	L	M	H	H	H	H	M	M
25=	61	Monsanto Co.	pharmaceuticals vs chemical vs agricultural products vs food products	M	H	M	H	H	H	H	H
25=	32	Motorola Inc.	semiconductor products vs consumer & light industrial subsystems	H	H	H	H	H	H	M	M
25=	54	Nations Bank Corp.	general banking vs financial services vs global banking	M	L	H	H	H	H	M	M
25=	52	Nynex	network + wireless telecoms vs cable video	L	L	L	H	H	H	L	L
25=	5	Philip Morris Inc.	tobacco vs food + beer	M	H	M	L	M	M	M	M
25=	88	Raytheon	engineering and construction vs aircraft + electronics vs aircraft	L	L	H	H	M	H	L	L
25=	90	Rockwell International	electronics + aerospace vs automotive	H	M	M	M	M	M	H	M
25=	68	Sara Lee Corp.	packaged meat and bakery vs household and body care vs personal products	M	H	H	H	H	H	M	M
25=	65	Time Warner	publishing vs entertainment	M	M	H	H	H	H	H	H
25=	84	United Technologies	elevators + heating and ventilation vs flight systems + aircraft engines + automotive parts	M	M	H	H	H	H	M	M

185

Breakup Rank	Size Rank	Company Name	Chosen Business Unit Comparison	Management	Customers	Technology/ Manufacturing	Buying	Intertrading	Brand/ Image	Differences Score
43=	33	Abbott Laboratories	pharmaceutical & nutritional vs hospital & laboratory	H	M	H	H	M	H	H
43=	37	Boeing Co.	commercial aircraft vs defense & space	M	M	L	M	H	H	L
43=	31	Citicorp	consumer banking vs commercial banking	M	H	H	L	H	H	M
43=	12	Hewlett-Packard Co.	computer products + electronic instruments vs chemical analysis	H	H	H	H	H	H	H
43=	50	Kimberly-Clark	personal care + tissue products vs newsprint	H	H	M	L	H	M	M
43=	40	Minnesota Mining & Manufacturing Co.	industrial & consumer products vs life sciences	L	H	L	M		H	M
43=	22	Pfizer Inc.	pharmaceuticals vs animal health	H	H	L	M	H	H	M
43=	51	Schering Plough Corp.	pharmaceuticals vs healthcare products	M	M	L	M	H	H	L
51=	3	AT&T Corp.	fixed telecoms vs cellular vs on-line services	L	M	L	L	H	M	L
51=	39	Bell Atlantic Corp.	network + wireless telecoms vs cable video	L	M	L	L	H	M	L
51=	64	Chase Manhattan Corp.	commercial banking vs investment services	L	L	M	M	H	L	L
51=	98	Colgate Palmolive Co.	personal care vs household products	L	H	M	M	H	H	M
51=	97	General Re Corp.	re-insurance vs derivatives dealing	M	M	M	M	H	H	M
51=	56	Sears	retailing vs mail order vs car servicing	M	M	H	M	L	L	M
57	80	US West Inc.	media group vs communications	M	L	M	H	L	H	L
58=	79	Union Pacific Corp.	railroad vs trucking	L		H			M	
58=	15	Walt Disney Co.	film entertainment + retailing vs theme park resorts	M	L	H	H	M	L	L
60=	36	Ameritech	telecoms vs cable TV	M	L	L	H	H	H	L
60=	66	First Union Corp.	retail banking vs commercial banking	M	H	L	L	H	H	L
60=	21	GTE Corp.	fixed telecoms vs cellular telecoms	M	M	L	L	H	M	M
60=	34	SBC Communications Inc.	fixed telecoms vs cellular telecoms	L	M		L		M	L
60=	48	Texaco Inc.	exploration & production + refining marketing & distribution vs non-petroleum	M		H	H	H	L	
65=	96	Automatic Data Processing Inc.	brokerage services vs dealer services	L	H	L	M	L	M	M
65=	82	Caterpillar	engines vs machines + financial services	L	H	M	M	H	M	L
65=	87	May Department Stores Co.	department stores vs shoe stores	L	L	L	L	H	H	L
65=	94	Norwest	banking vs mortgage banking vs Norwest financial	L	L	M	L	M	M	L
65=	11	Wal-Mart Stores Inc.	Wal-Mart stores vs Sam's clubs	L	L	L	M	M	H	L

186

Rank	No.	Company	Segment							
70=	24	BellSouth Corp.	fixed telecoms vs cellular telecoms	L	M	H	L	L	M	L
70=	57	MCI Communications Corp.	mobile vs fixed phones	L	M	H	M	M	L	L
70=	81	Xerox	personal copying and printing vs document outsourcing + production publishing	L	M	M	M	L	M	M
73=	10	Procter & Gamble Inc.	laundry & cleaning + personal hygiene + beauty care + healthcare vs food + beverage	L	H	H	H	M	L	L
73=	55	Travelers Group	investment services vs life insurance vs property and casualty insurance services	L	M	H	H	M	L	M
75	42	Columbia/HCA Healthcare Corp.	hospitals + outpatient centers vs home healthcare	L	M	L	H	H	L	L
76=	58	Allstate	(single segment)	na	na	na	na	na	na	na
76=	63	Anheuser-Busch Companies Inc.	(single segment)	na	na	na	na	na	na	na
76=	92	Baxter International	(single segment)	na	na	na	na	na	na	na
76=	89	Burlington Northern	(single segment)	na	na	na	na	na	na	na
76=	71	Campbell Soup Co.	(single segment)	na	na	na	na	na	na	na
76=	45	Chrysler Corp.	(single segment)	na	na	na	na	na	na	na
76=	2	Coca-Cola Co.	(single segment)	na	na	na	na	na	na	na
76=	62	Computer Associates International Inc.	(single segment)	na	na	na	na	na	na	na
76=	30	Eli Lilly & Co.	(single segment)	na	na	na	na	na	na	na
76=	29	Federal National Mortgage Association	(single segment)	na	na	na	na	na	na	na
76=	77	Freddie Mac	(single segment)	na	na	na	na	na	na	na
76=	43	Home Depot Inc.	(single segment)	na	na	na	na	na	na	na
76=	14	Intel Corp.	(single segment)	na	na	na	na	na	na	na
76=	74	JP Morgan	(single segment)	na	na	na	na	na	na	na
76=	67	Kellogg	(single segment)	na	na	na	na	na	na	na
76=	26	McDonald's Corp.	(single segment)	na	na	na	na	na	na	na
76=	6	Merck & Co.	(single segment)	na	na	na	na	na	na	na
76=	9	Microsoft Corp.	(single segment)	na	na	na	na	na	na	na
76=	99	Nike	(single segment)	na	na	na	na	na	na	na
76=	49	Oracle Corp.	(single segment)	na	na	na	na	na	na	na
76=	100	Pacific Telesis Group	(single segment)	na	na	na	na	na	na	na
76=	53	Pharmacia Upjohn Inc.	(single segment)	na	na	na	na	na	na	na
76=	72	Southern Co.	(single segment)	na	na	na	na	na	na	na
76=	91	Sprint	(single segment)	na	na	na	na	na	na	na
76=	75	WMX Technologies Inc.	(single segment)	na	na	na	na	na	na	na

Historical Example Breakups : Overall Breakup Index Ranking and Scores

Company	Chosen Business Unit Comparison	SBU Differences	ROS Differential	Annual Report Rationale	Share Performance	Brokers Report	Total Score (%)
Corning	lab services vs spec materials vs comms vs cons prods	M	H	H	H	H	90
Lonhro	hotels vs mining	H	H	H	H	M	90
Hanson	overall	H	H	H	M	M	90
ITT	insurance vs industrial vs hosp/ent vs comms/info	H	H	H	M	H	90
Thorn EMI	Thorn vs EMI	H	H	H	M	H	90
British Gas	gas supply vs gas distribution	M	H	H	M	H	80
Racal	security (Chubb) vs telecoms vs data/network	M	M	H	M	H	80
PepsiCo Inc.	beverages + snack foods vs restaurants	M	H	H	H	H	80
AT&T	telecom systems & services vs computers	M	M	H	M	H	80
Tenneco	automotive vs energy vs packaging vs shipbuilding	H	M	H	M	L	70
ICI	bioscience vs industrial chems/spec chems/mats	M	L	L	M	M	70
Marriott	food concessions vs hotels vs real estate	M	M	H	na	L	63
Sears Roebuck	stores/storecard vs insurance/financial services	H	M	M	H	L	60
3M	industrial/consumer vs data storage vs life sciences	H	L	H	H	L	60
General Mills	consumer foods vs restaurants	H	M	H	H	L	60
General Motors	EDS vs rest (automotive/financial/etc.)	H	L	H	H	L	60
English China Clays	clays vs construction material	M	M	H	H	L	60
Eli Lilly	medical devices vs pharmaceuticals	M	na	H	M	L	50
Baxter International	medical technology vs healthcare mngt vs med. distribution	M	na	H	M	L	40
Monsanto Co.	pharmaceuticals vs chemicals vs agricultural products vs food products	M	M	H	M	L	50
WR Grace	healthcare vs packaging/catalysts/water treat chems/ construction mats	M	M	M	L	H	50
BAT	tobacco vs retail vs paper vs financial services	H	M	H	L	L	50
Rockwell International	electronics + aerospace vs automotive	H	H	M	L	L	50
American Brands	spirits + hardware + home improvement vs tobacco	M	M	M	H	L	50
Courtaulds	chems, materials/coatings/films/fibers vs /textiles	M	L	H	M	L	40
Pacific Telesis	fixed vs cellular	L	na	H	M	L	38

Index